Conversations with John Searle

An interview by **Gustavo Faigenbaum**

Design, typesetting, and other prepress work by Libros en Red
www.librosenred.com

Printed in U.S.A.

ISBN: 987-1022-11-5

First english edition - Print on Demand

LibrosEnRed
A trade mark of Amertown International S.A.
editorial@librosenred.com

Conversations with John Searle

An interview by **Gustavo Faigenbaum**

Gustavo Faigenbaum

Publisher:

A Trade Mark of
Amertown International S.A.

www.librosenred.com

Cover and Interior Design: Patricio Olivera

Communication Manager: Andrés Rivas

C.E.O. Marcelo Perazolo

Published by LibrosEnRed
editorial@librosenred.com
www.librosenred.com

Table of Contents

Acknowledgments

First of all, I would like to thank **John Searle** for having accepted to participate in this project. I must also mention his extraordinary hospitality and his disposition to read, and make suggestions on, a previous version of this text.

The idea to do and publish these interviews came up during a conversation with **Dr. María Ignacia Massone**. She contacted Prof. Searle, and invited me to include this volume in the Semiotics and Philosophy Series she directs in **LibrosEnRed.com**. A special note of gratitude to her for this initiative.

Before flying to Berkeley I engaged in an exchange of ideas with some philosophers and intellectuals, who suggested problems and issues to be explored in my meetings with Searle. Special thanks to **Diego Lawler**, **Greg Klass**, **Ricardo Minervino**, **Juan A. Samaja**, **María Ignacia Massone** and **José A. Castorina**, for their collaboration in the formulation and selection of the questions.

Gustavo Faigenbaum

Intellectual biography

"A remarkable intellectual atmosphere"

G. F.:

Where were you born?

John Searle:

I was born in 1932 on July 31st in Denver, Colorado. My mother was a doctor and so she could pretty much choose whichever hospital I was going to be born in. I was actually born in a sanitarium - Porter Sanitarium in Denver. My father was an electrical engineer who worked for the telephone company. He was an engineer for the Mountain State Telephone Company, which was a branch of AT&T. And then I grew up in Denver until the Second World War

Because of the war a lot of people were moved around in the United States. My father was transferred to the headquarters of AT&T in New York. And so we moved to the New York area and lived in a suburb of New York in Short Hills, New Jersey. And my mother worked at a hospital in New

York, at Bellevue Hospital, as a doctor. My father worked in the Wall Street area for AT&T, which was then the world's biggest private corporation.

G. F.:

I've read that you went to a special school in New York.

John Searle:

Yes. I did. When we lived in New York I went to an experimental school run by Columbia University called Horace Man-Lincoln, which was the original John Dewey School. It was the experimental school of the Columbia Teachers' College and it was a remarkable school. The Teachers College lost so much money on it that eventually they just abolished it. The tuition we paid was nowhere near enough to cover the cost of it. I don't know how valuable it was as a source of educational experiment, given the fact that the students were so unusual. They were selected from all over the City of New York and it was by competitive examination that one could get admission to the school.

My parents were convinced that they ought always to get me into the best possible schools and this was the best school in New York, I believe. It was a very intense intellectual atmosphere.

Unfortunately, my mother caught a disease from one of her patients and she died just at that time - she died the same day the atomic bomb was dropped on Hiroshima. I had just turned 13. So, anyway, after the war, my father was transferred to Wisconsin and remarried. I finished my high school education in Wisconsin and graduated from Shorewood High School.

G. F.:

I guess it was probably unusual at that time for a woman to be a doctor.

John Searle:

Very unusual. My mother graduated from medical school in 1930 and, if you look at the photograph of her graduating class, there were only two women in the whole class. It was very unusual and very difficult to have a career as a doctor because there was a great deal of discrimination against women and, incidentally, discrimination by other women. Other women often wouldn't go to a woman doctor. In school, the women teachers would refuse to believe that my mother was a doctor. They'd say, "No, you must mean she's a nurse." They wouldn't believe it when they asked, "What does your mother do?" and I would say that

11

she's a doctor. I held my ground and pointed out, "No, she's not a nurse. She's a doctor." But that was unusual at that period in history. Now it's very common, of course.

G. F.:

Did the fact that your mother was a professional medical doctor made you more open-minded, in the sense of thinking of women as equal members of the profession?

John Searle:

I think probably. I now realize that was an unusual environment in Denver because both my parents were highly educated, I had a mother who was active in the medical profession, and we had a house full of people who were more intellectual, certainly, than the average household. My parents' friends included psychoanalysts who had been trained by Freud, who had escaped from Hitler and had moved to Denver. I remember there was one communist who used to come to the house regularly. That was unusual.

G. F.:

"Here comes the communist!"

John Searle:

Well, nobody described him that way, but I was told he was a member of the Communist Party. It was an unusual environment in that respect. So, I didn't lack for intellectual stimulation. Even at Shorewood High School, though I thought the high school education was very routine and conventional, I had a lot of friends who were intellectually inclined. So I never for a moment doubted that my primary interests were intellectual, even when I was 14 or 15 years old.

"I had an unusual bunch of friends in high school and in college. And we were, now that I think about it, for sixteen-year-olds, we were pretty self-consciously intellectual. That is, we hated American popular culture. We had nothing to do with the culture of the fifties. We threw up when we heard Bing Crosby or Frank Sinatra. We thought that was just dreck, we wanted nothing to do with that. And we were self-consciously intellectual in our interests, and I think that was healthy."

From John Searle Interview: Conversations with History; Institute of International Studies, UC Berkeley. (http://globetrotter.berkeley.edu/people/Searle/searle-con0.html)

G. F.:

What college did you attend?

Gustavo Faigenbaum

John Searle:

Well, I was only 16 when I graduated from high school. My father wanted me to go to Princeton, and I suppose I should have done that, but I was very depressed and unhappy, and I decided to go to the University of Wisconsin. I went to the University of Wisconsin, really, because it was convenient. A lot of my friends were going there and it was only an hour or two drive from where I lived in Milwaukee. In the end, it turned out to be a great educational experience for me, because they had a special program called Integrated Liberal Studies and they tried, for the first two years, to integrate the three major areas of investigation–the natural sciences, the social sciences and the humanities. And in addition to these three courses, students also took a course in English where they had to write essays for the other three subjects. And, of course, the integration was not intellectually successful because they were actually quite different areas of investigation. But, *educationally*, it was a great success. For the first time, I got a sense of intellectual history going from the Greeks to the present. And I got a sense of science as an activity that human beings engage in as part of intellectual endeavor. And though the social science part of this was probably the weakest, in the social science courses I did get a sense of history, a sense of

14

historical change and development. And maybe one of the most important things I got, which I think any intellectual has to have, is the capacity to see yourself as part of history, as caught up in the cross-currents of historical development. So, my first two years at Wisconsin were very intellectually intense and that was a marvelous experience. I think I got a better education in those two years than most of my friends who went to more prestigious universities.

Then at the end of my second year I did something that really changed my life. I got a job on a boat with a friend of mine, and we worked our way over to Europe. This was a boat that had been chartered for the Council on Student Travel. I worked in the kitchen.

G. F.:

What year was that?

John Searle:

This would be 1951. When we got to Europe we just hitchhiked around and traveled around Europe. We went to Paris for the first month and then traveled around for the rest of the summer, hitchhiking around. Much of the time I was alone. I came back on the sister ship of this boat at the end

15

of the summer and went back to Wisconsin. But I was determined then that I wanted to go to Europe. I wanted to be a student in Europe. Back in Wisconsin I discovered that I wasn't really eligible. I was only a 19-year-old junior. I was only eligible to apply for a Rhodes scholarship, because for all of the other scholarships you had to be older, you had to be a senior and ready to do graduate work. So I applied for the Rhodes scholarship and I got it. That was a great thing for me.

G. F.:

Did you have very high grades?

John Searle:

I was not a superstar, in any sense, in high school. I did all right, but nothing unusual. I was very nervous when I got to Wisconsin. I wasn't sure that I could succeed, so I worked hard. I got straight A's and also became President of the student body. I became President of the student government when I was 18.

G. F.:

What got you involved in school politics?

John Searle:

Someone suggested to me that I should run for the student government and I did. I was very nervous and insecure about that. So I tried very hard and I succeeded spectacularly. I got a lot of people to vote for me. So I then went the next step and became President of the whole student government. But it didn't really mean anything to me. My real passion was for intellectual values. So I did something that was unheard of. I resigned. I resigned my position as student body President because I really wanted to pursue my intellectual interests. I didn't want to make a lot of speeches and attend a lot of meetings. I wanted to read a lot of books and get a lot of ideas, so I quit. And I haven't really pursued politics professionally since then, although I was very active in the revolution in Berkeley, in the Free Speech Movement. At that time I devoted about three years of my life to political activities, but it was of an unconventional variety. It wasn't a matter of running for office and having a political campaign.

Anyway, back in Wisconsin I had, on paper at least, an unusual CV, an unusual dossier, and that impressed the people who gave these scholarships and I got a scholarship to Oxford.

17

Gustavo Faigenbaum

G. F.:

Had you already decided that you wanted to do philosophy?

John Searle:

No. I hadn't really. I hadn't decided what I wanted to do. My great love was literature. And, in fact, I spent a whole month in my junior year learning Joyce's Ulysses. And I really got to know that book. Not by heart, but I knew every development in it, and I knew how it compared with the Odyssey. I had very good professors. My professors were really good people, who taught me just for fun. It wasn't a regular course; I was interested in the book, and my professors were anxious to help me.

So I'd have to say my great love was literature in those days. I loved philosophy, but it seemed to me a lot of it was hard to understand and I couldn't see the point of a lot of the authors, like Leibniz and Spinoza, for example. So I didn't really become committed to the study of philosophy until I got to Oxford.

The Oxford Years

John Searle

I didn't travel with the other Rhodes scholars. But, to save money, I traveled to Oxford, again, on a boat where I was employed. I arrived in Oxford, left my trunk, and again traveled around Europe for the summer. I went back to Oxford in the fall of 1952. That year was when I began to become interested in philosophy. I didn't go to Oxford because it was especially good in philosophy. It was only after I was there that I found it was the center, it was the world's best place for philosophy at that time.

G. F.:

So you didn't really have any idea of what was going on there before you arrived?

John Searle:

No. Most of the people that I subsequently worked with I had never heard of. I had heard of Gilbert Ryle because my best teacher in Wisconsin was Julius Weinberg and he had told me that I should get in touch with Gilbert Ryle. But his lectures were disappointing. They were very slow, they had very little content, and they were addressed at a very low level.

My first year there was more or less disappointing. I mean, I had to study British constitutional history. I had to take the preliminary exams because I had no degree. I had to start from the beginning, like the other freshmen. I had to take exams in French, in British constitutional history and in economics. It didn't hurt me to do that, but my first year at Oxford was not really an intense intellectual experience. It was only at the end of my first year that I started to do philosophy and I met other undergrads that were also interested in philosophy.

Let me explain a little bit about Oxford because it's not a regular university. The basic teaching of undergraduates is done in tutorials. You write an essay each week for your tutor.

You have three terms in a year, and each term lasts 8 weeks. In any term you will study two subjects. So you'd write two essays a week. In my case, I might do an essay in philosophy and an essay in economics each week. You'd bring your essay to your tutor and you'd read it aloud and then the tutor would criticize it and discuss it.

The basic part of your education as a student is the tutorial system. Now, in addition to that, there are lectures. You go to the lectures really for supplement, for entertainment, for inspiration, for amusement. But the bulk of the work that you do, you'd do it by yourself in a library, preparing your essays. And then you'd go to lectures to supplement this.

There were also graduate seminars, but often undergraduates would be prevented from going to seminars if the seminars were crowded.

The faculty was divided into two kinds: the college tutors who worked for the colleges, and the professors, who did not tutor undergraduates but lectured to the whole University. There were only three professors in philosophy - Austin, Ryle and Price. There were 60 or 65 philosophy tutors spread throughout the university, who might also give lectures. You didn't get to know the professors well while you were an undergraduate. The only exception to that was that the professors did hold informal instruction for undergraduates, and I went to Austin's informal instruction.

I did go to a lot of lectures. But I also have to say that I think the most intense philosophical education was arguing philosophy with my fellow undergraduates. There was an intense group of

21

Gustavo Faigenbaum

people who were passionately interested in philosophy, who were students at the time. It included many people who later became well known, like Ronald Dworkin, Charles Taylor, Frank Cioffi, and David Wiggins. We were all undergraduates together. And then there were others who were good at philosophy, but who went on and did other things like Nigel Lawson, who became Chancellor of the Exchequer.

G. F.:

People like Charles Taylor or Ronald Dworkin are not average philosophers. I think they all have in common certain wideness in their views; they have written works that span over many subjects.

John Searle:

Right. Ronny Dworkin was always interested in politics and law. And Charles had a very deep interest in politics and political philosophy. In fact, he was active in Canadian politics for a while, and actually ran for political office. So, Oxford was often said to be very narrow, and in a way it was, because we were obsessed with language. But, in fact, it was not as narrow as people make it out to be.

G. F.:

Was Georg Von Wright also at Oxford?

John Searle:

No. Von Wright was not in Oxford at the time and as far as I know I've never met him. I have corresponded with him and he seems to be a very nice man. He's a very civilized, intelligent man. He had been at Cambridge and had been close to Wittgenstein. There is a paradox in his life, in that of the people who were close to Wittgenstein, he was probably the most intelligent. He really was a superior philosophical intellect. But he didn't think at all like Wittgenstein. His whole approach to philosophy is quite different from Wittgenstein's, the method is totally different, and so it's not at all clear to me what kind of a relationship they had. And I'm not sure about this, but I think Wittgenstein actually admired Von Wright more than any of his other students.

G. F.:

What about Stephen Toulmin?

Gustavo Faigenbaum
John Searle:

Yes. He was in Oxford and I actually attended his lectures. He was an Oxford Don. I don't know what his title was, but he did give lectures at Oxford and I did go to his lectures. They were about reasoning and I thought they were disappointing. I mean, they were like John Dewey. They were sort of, well, this is pragmatic and we'll just use it because it's useful this way. He gave the lectures in Oxford that later became *The Uses of Argument*. [1]

G. F.:

And you are not sympathetic to his approach.

John Searle:

I'm not, no. It would be a little bit hard after all these years to try to remember it, but the way I remember it, it was in the style of pragmatism. Where you just think, "this is a useful way to proceed." Whereas my own view is that there are criteria of what's right and wrong, what's true and false, what's valid and invalid. And that these are not, so to speak, up for grabs. We're not in a situation where anything goes.

---

[1] TOULMIN, STEPHEN E. *The Uses of Argument*. Cambridge: Cambridge University Press, 1958.

G. F.:

Yes, but I think that his claim that traditional logic has been fascinated with a geometrical ideal is very interesting. He attempts to explain why logic cannot give an account of the kind of reasoning we use in everyday situations. And so he takes up the idea of "good form", or "good procedure," which he imports from juridical or legal contexts. For instance, when you go to court you have to keep with certain formalities. And I thought that in a way that move was similar to Austin's, at least to Austin's understanding of the formal features of speech acts in terms of felicity conditions, which are formal criteria, but are not strictly logical criteria.

John Searle:

Well, that's interesting and that may be the right way to look at it. But when it came to questions like truth, Austin was in no sense a relativist, and he believed in the correspondence theory of truth and, though I never talked to him about logical validity, I think that he would similarly have a fairly strict attitude. I never thought that you might do an analogy between Toulmin's approach and Austin's.

By the way, you know, Toulmin married John Austin's sister. There's a famous story about how Toulmin once addressed Austin by his first name.

25

This did not go over very well with Austin. Austin said, according to people present, "Austin is also a Christian name." Meaning "you should address me as Austin."

Anyway, this was a very exciting time to be in Oxford and there were a·lot of very good people who covered all sorts of different aspects of philosophy. It wasn't just ordinary language philosophy, but there were people like Isaiah Berlin and Stuart Hampshire, who were interested in other parts of philosophy besides ordinary language. There were also people who had more interest in logic, like Michael Dummett. So I had a broad education in philosophy, in the sense that there was never a party line. It was never ideologically as narrow as people sometimes pretend that Oxford was.

Searle (center) celebrating the end of exams at Oxford, June 1955

My education did have peculiar holes. I never really learned the history of philosophy. I was doing a degree in Philosophy, Politics and Economics, P.P.E., which was a regular cluster of subjects. We didn't do much philosophy before Descartes. I did learn the history of modern philosophy, especially Descartes, Locke, Berkeley and Hume. But I didn't learn any Kant or Leibniz or Spinoza, and I certainly didn't learn very much Plato or Aristotle.

G. F.:

You weren't required to learn ancient Greek or Latin?

John Searle:

No. I would have been if I had taken the other philosophy program, which was called *Greats*, or *Literae Humanioraes*. And there you had to know Greek. In PPE, I did have to master Plato's *Theatetus*, and Aristotle's *Categories* and *De Interpretatione*. But basically, in the history of the subject, I was very poorly trained, and I am to this day. I don't really know much about the history of philosophy. I think it's probably just as well. I think my career would have been different if I had spent a lot of time trying to master historical characters.

27

G. F.:

And there is a certain weight of tradition...

John Searle:

That's right. And I never felt that. I never felt any weight of tradition bearing down on me.

G. F.:

Has the fact that you started doing philosophy by working on ordinary language determined your general frame of mind? For instance, would you say that your habit of comparing philosophical insights with everyday intuitions comes from there?

John Searle:

I don't think so. I was never really one of the religious fanatics about ordinary language in Oxford. Oddly enough, I never thought of myself at Oxford as a follower of Austin. Austin had many followers. In fact, there were many debates among the students as to how good his work was and whether or not he was really the best. People had varying opinions about Austin's project. I was never fully a supporter of the project that you could solve all or most philosophical problems by attending to the use of words. Now in his official moments,

Austin himself never said that. He always said, "This is one way of doing philosophy, there are of course other ways." But at times he would also say things like, "There are about a thousand philosophical problems left and if we really got to work we ought to be able to solve all of them." I never believed that – that we could make a list, assign different people jobs, and we'd go out and solve all the problems. We could have a division of labor and we would go out and solve all philosophical problems. I never believed that.

However, I did get one thing in Oxford, although it may have been something I had already: the feeling that you better not say anything that's obviously false. If somebody tells you that we can never really know how things are in the real world, or that consciousness doesn't exist, or that we really can't communicate with each other, or that you can't mean "rabbit" when you say "rabbit," I know that's false. I know if you get a ridiculous result, you made a mistake and you better go back and find the mistake. You don't say anything that is ridiculous. That sort of stuff that you get in Derrida and people like that. I was never, in any way, tempted to that.

So it wasn't so much ordinary language, but just sheer respect for facts. Just the sheer basic facts of how the world is and how it works. That's the first

Gustavo Faigenbaum

thing. And then the second thing is, in Oxford I got a kind of self confidence that I could do this, and that you needn't be intimidated by the fact that there are all these people who have huge reputations, and know so much, and know so many languages, and have read a lot of Plato and Aristotle, and know mathematical logic. And it's easy for young philosophers to be intimidated by the burden of the history of the subject and the technical character of many of the questions, and the distinction of the existing workers in the field. I was never scared by any of that.

I was to some extent intimidated by the fact that I wasn't very good at mathematics and I thought, "Well, I'll never be able to do the kinds of things that Frege and Russell did." But even that, I'm not so much afraid of anymore. I've written an article about the philosophy of mathematics, and what numbers are. So, I did get two things at Oxford, even though and I don't know if I got them there, or if I had them before and that was; 1) a sheer respect for the facts, and 2) a certain amount of self-confidence, that I could actually do this subject. And those are things that I try to give my students. A sense that "you can do this." It's something that's done by a lot of famous people, but you do it anyway. And secondly, when you do it you better respect the facts. You better not say anything that's just plain, obviously false. You make enough mistakes

30

anyway, but don't start off with some ridiculous falsehood.

John Austin

John Searle:

Austin, who had a big influence on me, regarded the history of philosophy mostly as a history of confusion. He used to describe it as, "All that old stuff!" Now, he thought that if we were going to do this kind of philosophy, we had to do it with impeccable scholarship. He thought that if you were going to write about Leibniz you have to know Leibniz's works better than Leibniz himself. But he didn't think that was the exciting part of philosophy. He thought the exciting part of philosophy was contemporary philosophy, and especially the investigation of ordinary language.

G. F.:

When did you meet John Austin?

John Searle:

It was during my second year at Oxford. I had heard Austin was very famous so I went to some lectures. They were about speech acts and I

31

thought it was all very boring. I thought it was so boring that I stopped going (laughing). So it wasn't until later that I realized, no, there's something interesting here. In fact, Austin inspired my first book and I eventually became a professional in the field of speech acts. But when I first heard Austin lecture about speech acts I did not think that it could be important or that it could be interesting. I just thought it was dull. I stopped going because he seemed to be fussing about all these English verbs and it didn't really seem to be getting to the real meat of the philosophy. So it wasn't until my second year at Oxford that I really began to be seriously interested in philosophy, and to seriously think about pursuing it as a career.

G. F.:

Had you heard about Wittgenstein before getting to Oxford?

John Searle:

I didn't really *know* about Wittgenstein. I had heard the name, but Wittgenstein died in 1951, and I didn't arrive in England until 1952. So it was really after his death that I found about Wittgenstein. I never met Wittgenstein, but I did meet a lot of his students, like Elizabeth Anscombe and Yorick Smythies, and various other people.

When I first tried to study Wittgenstein, I insisted that we study it with Austin. Austin was hopeless with Wittgenstein because he was unsympathetic.

G. F.:

Was that the *Tractatus*?

John Searle:

No. The *Philosophical Investigations* had just come out and this was in 1953 or 1954.

G. F.:

Seen in a historical perspective, Austin and the later Wittgenstein always seemed to me to share a common attitude, and a whole set of similar core assumptions.

John Searle:

There are, as Wittgenstein would say, family resemblances. But Austin's style of philosophy was profoundly opposed to Wittgenstein's. Wittgenstein was often obscure, oracular; and he spoke in this grand style. Austin thought it was all very confused.

Gustavo Faigenbaum

Austin's approach to Wittgenstein was very unsympathetic. He insisted on taking everything absolutely literally. So if Wittgenstein said, "Well, suppose everyone has a beetle in the box," Austin said, "Next week everyone bring a box with a beetle in it." Now he meant that sarcastically, but that was his approach. And when we went over that passage he said, "Look, Wittgenstein is just contradicting himself. First he says everybody's got a beetle in his box and then later on he says maybe the box is empty. It's a plain contradiction." So, Austin was very unsympathetic to *Witters* (pronounced *Vitters*), as he called him, you know, in his English schoolboy slang.

And maybe the most unintelligent thing I ever heard Austin say about Wittgenstein was: "It's all in Moore!" He thought all of Wittgenstein's ideas were in G. E. Moore. Austin admired Moore because Moore was careful and cautious and tried to speak the truth and speak it clearly. Austin learned nothing from Wittgenstein; and he didn't like Wittgenstein's followers in Oxford either. Especially Elizabeth Anscombe. He referred to her as "that ninny."

G. F.:

So would you say that there was no influence of one on the other?

34

John Searle:

I think not. I think they were both part of a movement in Britain, and indeed in Europe generally, that emphasized language. It came to Austin by way of Prichard, Cook Wilson, Moore, and Russell. Russell influenced Moore, and Moore influenced Austin. But I don't think Austin learned much of anything from Wittgenstein. And I'm certain Wittgenstein didn't learn anything from Austin. Wittgenstein and Ryle were close at one time, but Ryle and Austin weren't all that close.

G. F.:

It's ironic that sometimes, when scholars try to present a pragmatic approach to language, they put Austin and Wittgenstein together.

John Searle:

That's a confusion. Austin really thought: if we're going to make progress in philosophy, the way to do it is to examine the ordinary use of English expressions, especially English verbs.

Now, I thought there were other ways of doing philosophy. I didn't think that was the only way of doing it, but he thought that was the most fruitful way at this particular phase in history, and it's what

35

he knew how to do. And he tried to be very careful at it. He was constantly telling me that he thought I should spend more time on particular verbs, speech act verbs for example.

G. F.:

Did you get this type of training with him? Like opening a dictionary on a random page, picking out a word, and discussing what it meant?

John Searle:

Yes. Austin's style in conversation was very precise. So once I used the word "suppose" and he said, "what does the 'sup' mean in suppose?" I mean, he thought we ought to have that kind of detailed knowledge every step of the way. Austin would stop in the conversation and say, "Why did you use the subjunctive?" He was very precise in niceties of ordinary usage, both in ordinary conversation and in his professional work. There was nothing loose or relaxed about Austin. In fact, Austin's most savage criticism of anything would be to say, "It's just loose!" And he thought that was the worst crime a philosopher could commit. He used to shake his head sadly and say, "There's a lot of loose thinking in this town." As if this was a terrible problem we had, all this loose thinking going on all over Oxford, and there's nothing we could do to stop it. So Austin was very much in favor of a great deal of precision and he felt this was the way to make progress in philosophy.

> I once asked him: "how soon can we hope that your William James' lectures will be published?" thus giving him an opening I should never have done. He responded immediately, "You can *hope* it will be published any time you like"
> From John Searle's article on *John Langshaw Austin*

G. F.:

Now, to summarize the contrast with Wittgenstein...

John Searle:

Well, I think Wittgenstein really thought the point of examining ordinary language was to solve traditional philosophical problems. He thought that, if you see how the language game is played, then you will no longer be tempted toward a skeptical conclusion. But Austin wanted to go to the next step. He thought ordinary language was absolutely fascinating as a field of research in it's own right. And we weren't trying so much to solve philosophical problems when we did the theory of speech acts, but we were trying to, in effect, create a new branch of philosophy.

37

Now there's an irony about Austin's life. During his life he had a reputation as someone who had no interest in a general theory, but was just interested in detailed minutia of linguistic distinctions. Now, in fact, I think his greatest contribution was the development of the beginning of the general theory of speech acts. When he was alive, people thought, "Not interested in generalities, only interested in specific details, but he's terrific on the details." In my experience, he got the details wrong a lot of the time, but he was a kind of genius at developing a general theory of language, and that's where he had the most profound influence on me.

But you see, he gave these lectures. And I used to argue with him after the lectures. In those days you didn't discuss something in the lecture. You didn't raise your hand and ask questions in the lecture. But after the lecture, I'd talk to him. He thought that his theory was, as he put it, too half-baked. I wanted him to publish it, because I wanted to criticize it, but he thought it was incomplete. He would not have published *How To Do Things With Words* in its present form if he had lived, because he didn't think it was good enough.

"Oxford had a long tradition of not publishing during one's lifetime, indeed it was regarded as slightly vulgar to publish (...) As far as having a career and making a reputation were

38

concerned, the attitude in Oxford was that the only opinions that really matter are the opinions of people in Oxford, and perhaps a few in Cambridge and London..."

"[Austin] was hated for much the same reason that Socrates was hated – he seemed to destroy everything without leaving anything substantive in its place. Like Socrates he challenged orthodoxy without presenting an alternative, and equally comforting, orthodoxy. All Austin offered, again like Socrates, was a new method for doing philosophy."

From John Searle's article on *John Langshaw Austin*

Peter Strawson

John Searle:

The best teacher I had as an undergraduate was Peter Strawson. Strawson really made a big difference in my life because he taught me how to do the subject at a high level. He tutored me for less than one term, but he did have a big impact on me. I saw in the way that he did philosophy a certain model of rational argument and careful assessment.

Peter Strawson was unusual in that he insisted to have my essays a day in advance, and he then read them himself and prepared comments on them. So it was not a typical tutorial. And, in fact, what was so unusual about Peter is that he would express my views better than I could. He'd ask me, "Now is this what you're trying to say?" And I would think, "Yes, that's exactly what I was trying to say. You said it better than I did." And then he'd proceed to show me that it was totally mistaken. He would say something like "there do appear to be four difficulties with this view" and then he'd annihilate it.

It was not easy being tutored by Peter Strawson. He could be absolutely devastating, but he was inspiring. I saw how you could do philosophy at a very high level.

So, the Oxford system of education is not like other universities. The basic heart of it is tutoring. My official tutor was Jim Urmson, but I was also tutored by other people. Urmson was pretty good, but I have to say my best tutor, by a long shot, was Peter Strawson.

Bertrand Russell

G. F.:

Did you ever meet Bertrand Russell?

John Searle:

I only met Russell once. When I was an undergraduate we had a society called the Voltaire Society. We used to have annual dinners either with Russell or Ayer, but the favorite ones were with Bertrand Russell. He was the patron of the Voltaire Society. And we would go off to London and have dinner at a restaurant in a private room. We were a bunch of undergraduates. And I was the President, I sat next to Russell and I talked to him all evening. It was quite interesting.

I remember that he felt that Wittgenstein's late work was just terrible. He thought it was a terrible falling off from the great work that he'd done as a young man. I asked him what he thought about the *Philosophical Investigations*, and I remember what he said verbatim. He said, "I don't think there's a word in it worth having been written." But he did preface it by saying, "I suppose I must be wrong about this." I mean, you'd have to imitate Russell's accent [with a strong British accent]: "I must be wrong about this, but I don't think there's a word in it worth having been written." And he was quite adamant that Wittgenstein had this terrible falling off, that he had stopped being a serious philosopher. "It's all pragmatics." For Russell it

41

was all kind of, you know, not serious logical studies.

And that's when he made his famous remark about God. Did I tell you about that? Russell was then 85 and, well, nobody's going to live forever. And we asked him, "You've been an atheist all your life. If you died and went to Heaven and it was true, they let you into Heaven, what would you say to Him? What would you say to God?" And he said, "I would say: *You didn't give us enough evidence.*" That was his attitude. He thought God had an epistemic job to do. If God exists, he is not doing his epistemic job. God should have given us more evidence.

Dagmar Carboch

G. F.:

What happened when your fellowship was over?

John Searle:

I had the Rhodes scholarship for three years and I finished my B.A. in 1955. I had to go to graduate school somewhere. I applied at various places in America and I was admitted. At that time, the best place to do the kind of philosophy I was interested in was Cornell. So I accepted Cornell. But I then applied for a scholarship at Oxford and I got it. I got a senior scholarship at St. Anthony's College, which was then a new college for graduate students only, so I decided to stay on at Oxford. Then during my first year of graduate work I got a job, and this was common in those days, you could get a job even with a B.A. I got a job as a Research Lecturer, what's called a Prize Fellow in other colleges.

G. F.:

Were you teaching classes?

John Searle:

No, I was a research lecturer of Christ Church and my responsibility was to tutor part-time. I taught a maximum of six hours a week and the rest of the time I did research. That's when I decided to do an Oxford D.Phil., which, is the equivalent of a Ph.D. I did the Oxford doctorate degree and that took me, in effect, the next three years after I got my job. So I was in Oxford for a total of seven years – three years as an undergraduate, one year as a graduate student at St. Anthony's, and three years again at Christ Church, my old college, as a *Don*, a faculty member.

G. F.:

Ok, what happened after you got your doctorate at Oxford? .

John Searle:

I had this job as a Research Lecturer at Christ Church, and I lived in college in a way that was typical of what we called "bachelor Dons". I had no wife, I lived in college, and I took all my meals there. They didn't pay me very much, but since I had a free place to live, I didn't need much to live. But then, I met a woman who was a refugee from Czechoslovakia. I met her in 1956, oddly enough in Austin's office. I met my wife, Dagmar, in Austin's office. He introduced me to her. She had just come from Australia.

G. F.:

So, Austin introduced you to your wife!

John Searle:

(Laughing) Yes, Austin had a bigger influence on me than I realized. He introduced me to my wife, he got me my first job at Berkeley, and he inspired

44

my first book. When he was alive I never really regarded myself, in any sense, as a follower of Austin. I thought I could beat him in argument. I thought the person I most admired was Peter Strawson, but I realize now that Austin had a bigger influence on me in the long run. And, certainly, he had a personal influence because he got me a job at Berkeley and he introduced me to a woman I later married.

But, in any case, Dagmar and I got married on Christmas Eve in 1958. And I needed more money, because I had to support a wife. And so I moved out of college and took a job as a full-time tutor of Christ Church, which was better paid.

Therefore, during my last year at Oxford I was a regular lecturer at Christ Church, not a research lecturer. But I knew I wanted to leave England, and Austin, in effect, arranged for me to come to Berkeley. I had other offers, for instance, I had an offer from Cornell. But Austin had been at Berkeley, and loved it, and thought it was a great place with a great future. So, in the summer of 1959, my wife and I came to Berkeley and we've lived here since.

"People didn't believe me when I told them I wasn't going to spend my life at Oxford: [with a heavy upper-crust British accent:] *Oh, that's frightfully amusing that you say that, but we*

45

Gustavo Faigenbaum

*don't take you seriously for a moment; we can't imagine you in
the United States. With whom would you possibly speak?"*

Extracted from "A conversation with John Searle"," *Carlifornia
Monthly,* February 1995

Dagmar did philosophy in Oxford and she got a
B-Phil degree. And when we came here, our hope
was that she could get a job teaching philosophy,
but there was discrimination against women then.
Her B-Phil was supposed to be a graduate teaching
degree in England, but the Americans had never
heard of it and didn't understand it, and they
thought she ought to get a Ph.D. In the end, what
she did was go into the law. And she did get a law
degree. She pursued a legal career. She's now
retired.

G. F.:

Are all your books dedicated to Dagmar?

John Searle:

I dedicated *The Campus War* and *Expression
and Meaning* to my two sons, Thomas and Mark. All
the other books are dedicated to Dagmar. And
there's no question that my wife is my chief
inspiration. I never publish anything unless she's
read it.

The Birth of Speech Acts

G. F.:

I assume that part of what you later published in *Speech Acts* was developed during the Oxford years.

John Searle:

Yes, but the great topic, the passionate subject in that period, was *reference*, and the theory of descriptions and proper names. And that's what my thesis was about: sense and reference. I wanted to embed that inside an account on speech acts, but it wasn't until later, after I left Oxford, that I really began to develop a general theory of speech acts.

In the 1960's I wrote an article called *What is a Speech Act?* and then a whole lot of things came clear to me. I then wrote the book *Speech Acts*. The materials in the thesis formed a kind of nucleus, the central chapters. [He gets up and looks for the doctoral thesis]. This is my thesis. And you can see there's a chapter on speech acts but, mostly, it's

47

about reference. And it was only after I came back to the United States that I began to take seriously the idea of developing a general account of speech acts.

G. F.:

So, there was a lot of Frege and Russell in there.

John Searle:

Exactly. Of the historical figures in philosophy, the biggest influence on the thesis was Frege. I wrote a very Fregean account of reference. My first published article was called "Proper Names." And it was, in effect, an essay I wrote for Peter Strawson. I had just finished my B.A. when I wrote the little essay on proper names and Peter said, "We'll send it to the journals and have them publish it," and so it was, although it took three years to get published.

John Searle:

When I came to Berkeley I was a beginning Assistant Professor. I was 26 years old when I left Oxford. I had a wife with a baby on the way. And we moved into an apartment in Berkeley Hills. I taught three courses a semester. That was pretty hard teaching then, because I taught a large lower division course, an upper division course, and a seminar every semester. I didn't, in fact, write very much during my first years in Berkeley; and I now think I was foolish not to.

Partly it was just arrogance. I had heard that the Americans had this system of "publish or perish" and I decided I wasn't going to do that. They were going to have to take me the way I was. But I would never publish anything if people thought it might be because I wanted to get promoted. I was what I was and I would do the work I did at my pace. And then I did go away a lot. I got offered a better job in Michigan and I went there for a year to try it, but my wife didn't like being in the Midwest, and I didn't like it either. We liked California better so we came back. And then in 1963 I got an American Council of Learned Societies' Study Fellowship to take a year off and study linguistics with Noam Chomsky at MIT and then go back to Oxford.

And that's really when I did a lot of writing. That was the academic year of 1963- 1964. I finished my book on speech acts in that period.

G. F.:

Did you actually work with Chomsky?

John Searle:

Yes. They were awfully good to me at MIT. They gave me an office – Chomsky had several offices. And we had countless discussions together, so I really got to know what Chomsky was doing then and what work was going on at MIT.

G. F.:

In Chomsky's *Reflections on Language*[2] I have read harsh criticisms of your theory of speech acts.

John Searle:

We have never agreed completely, and every time I have published a criticism of Noam, he has always published four or five replies to it. I mean, I've published criticisms in a book review, an article in the Times Literary Supplement, and then he replied to my criticisms in several books. So, Noam and I don't agree on certain fundamentals, but he was very helpful to me. They were very hospitable at MIT in accommodating my intellectual needs.

---

[2] Chomsky, N. (1998). Reflections on Language. New York: The New Press. (Original work published 1975).

The problem was that when I came back to Berkeley in 1964, the revolution broke out and I put the book aside and didn't work on it, I didn't finish it until 1967. And then it took the publishers forever. I submitted it in 1967 and it wasn't until the beginning of 1969 that they actually brought it out. Cambridge Press was very slow then. They were faster in the 17th century at producing a book than they were in the 1960's. And the reason was, of course, that they put you in a long line of books waiting to be published.

So, the publication of *Speech Acts* was delayed and, oddly enough, I thought, "Well, this book's coming out too late." When I finished it in 1964 that would have been the right time to publish it, but it came out five years too late. Well, in fact, it became a kind of classic. I mean, it was translated into a lot of languages. So it worked out all right.

Berkeley and the Free Speech Movement (FSM).

G. F.:

About your involvement in the Free Speech Movement, I find it interesting that, while working on speech acts, you were also concerned about free speech.

51

John Searle:

Well, let me talk a little bit about that. One of the reasons that I wanted to come back from England and live in the United States is that I wanted to be a member of a community and not an expatriate or a foreigner. This was especially difficult for me during the Suez Crisis of 1956. During that period there was a tremendous tension in England between the younger generation and the older generation. People of my generation felt that the involvement in the Suez battle was monstrous; that what the British government was doing was just terrible. We felt the way then that we felt later about the Americans in Vietnam, though it didn't last as long. But I felt as a foreigner that it was not really my position to become politically active: I thought, "I am here as a guest in this country."

So there were terrible fights in Oxford among Dons and I was involved in those fights at a personal level, but I didn't feel that I could do anything. I couldn't sign any petitions or engage in marches, or that sort of thing. I was just too circumspect, too principled to engage in something where I thought I would be over-extending the rights of a guest. So I wanted to go back and live in the

United States where I could be a full citizen and my children could grow up as citizens of the United States, and we could be full members of the community. And when I came back here I was active against the witch-hunts of the time of McCarthy.

I should mention that when I was a student at Wisconsin I had been Secretary of an organization called Students Against McCarthy. We were opposed to Senator McCarthy. Even as a 17, 18 year old I was active against McCarthy and in favor of free speech, the freedom of expression, and the freedom of association. So when I got back to California, I was also active against the equivalent of McCarthyism during the late 1950's and early 1960's. That was called the House UnAmerican Activities Committee, which, similarly, was trying to run these witch-hunts. They held sessions in San Francisco and I was in the demonstrations against these sessions. That was in May of 1960.

Later on, the House UnAmerican Activities Committee made a movie called Operation Abolition in which they tried to show that people like me had been either Communist agents or had been under the influence of Communist agents. I was outraged at this movie. So I made a speech against it when it was shown and, since I'm a good public speaker, I was asked by various people: "Would you be willing

53

to make a speech about this movie?" So I did. And then I got a call from a professor at the law school, an assistant professor like me. He wanted to show the movie and he wanted me to comment on the movie afterwards. Now, an hour before the movie was to be shown we received a call from the Chancellor's office saying that my speech would not be allowed. They said that it violated some University rule, that they hadn't been given seven days notice, that it was a controversial issue, that they required somebody on the other side, etc. But that was an outrage because I was a professor and those rules were never designed to apply to me.

These events had a profound influence on my life. I, a professor at the University of California, was forbidden to address students at the University of California when invited by another professor. So I had to address them at a fraternity house across the street, in a bar. This was an outrage.

G. F.:

Did you actually do that?

John Searle:

I did. I addressed them in the barroom. The students looked at me as if I was some dangerous Communist, some kind of dangerous radical. At that

54

point I knew the University of California was not committed to free speech. I didn't know what to do about this. I went to the various University committees and they, obviously, were just stonewalling me. They were just trying to cover this over. I was an Assistant Professor, I could easily be fired, and I had a wife and a baby. So I was in a very weak position to fight the University.

But, some years later – this was in 1961 that this incident happened –in 1964, a group of my students came to me and said, "The University is restricting our freedom of speech. Will you help us?" And they found in me a sympathetic audience.

So, I began making speeches on behalf of what came to be called the Free Speech Movement. And the Free Speech Movement was successful beyond the wildest expectations. Indeed, I should take you and show you some photographs that are over in Sproul Hall of me marching with the FSM.

It was a very intense time of my life. It had an unfortunate consequence, in that we succeeded far beyond any expectations that I ever had. And the result was that though we did get free speech, we managed to destroy the duly constituted authority. [Showing a photograph:] That's me right smack in the middle, right there. That is me.

Gustavo Faigenbaum

Searle (center) at Free Speech Movement rally, UC Berkeley, November 20, 1964

We had tremendous success, but beyond my expectations what happened was that we simply destroyed the official duly constituted authority of the University. We wiped out the Chancellor. There was no recognized authority. We produced a revolutionary situation in that the regular authorities had collapsed and there was a tremendous sense of possibility.

In a revolutionary situation, when the existing structure of authority collapses, there is an exhilarating sense of possibility. People feel like "we can remake this University to be something utopian". I never felt any of that. I was already 32 years old. So I thought that's a childish attitude. But

56

a lot of people felt like "this is going to be the greatest thing that ever happened". And I think people even thought "we were going to create a social revolution that will spread over the whole world and it's all going to start right here in Berkeley". I didn't think any of that. I wanted a first rate academic university.

When the new University administration came in, the Chancellor, Roger Heyns, in effect said to me: "You tore it down, now put it back together." We needed to restore the structure of authority in the University. And I spent two years of my life doing that. I did no research work at all.

G. F.:

That must have been very uncomfortable for you after participating in the FSM.

John Searle:

Very much so.

G. F.:

Now you'd have to stop the same people who had been on your side before.

Gustavo Faigenbaum

John Searle:

Many people felt I had betrayed the revolution. My own attitude is that the revolution had betrayed me. That I had certain specific goals, I achieved those goals, then stopped. No more. But a whole lot of people felt, "No, now we've achieved these goals, now we must go on. The movement must grow. We must have ever-new objectives, ever-new demands." And I saw it as damaging the intellectual structure of the University. And, essentially, I was alone. The conservative people hated me since they thought I was responsible for the revolution. The revolutionaries hated me because they thought I was a traitor. So I had a small number of friends in the University Administration that I worked with – the Chancellor, and the Vice Chancellor, and other friends. But, basically, I was somewhat isolated.

According to a young philosophy professor named John Searle, who has probably been the faculty member closest to the F.S.M., the problem should be stated another way. "The militants were forced into the leadership of the F.S.M. because of the intransigence of the administration on an issue on which they were clearly in the wrong," Searle says. "Of course these people are absolutists. They are radicals. They perform a useful function in society as gadflies, but they have no loyalty to the structure, and once you've forced the

58

population to adopt them as leaders, you have trouble. The problem is not how to handle them. The problem is how not to get in a position where a mass movement has to turn to them for leadership."

From "LETTER FROM BERKELEY", by Calvin Trillin. Published originally in The New Yorker, March 13, 1965

G. F.:

How did you manage to deal with that situation?

John Searle:

We drew the line and made it clear you can't go over this line. That is, if you go over this line we will respond. And one day I had the police arrest 11 friends of mine. That was very difficult.

G. F.:

To go over the line would be…?

John Searle:

To violate University rules. You have to say: "this is what you can do and this is what you can't do; this belongs to you, and this belongs to the University, and if you go over this line we will arrest you." And of the 11 arrested we got 10 convictions

59

in front of a Berkeley jury. That's amazing. I mean, it's very hard to get a conviction from Berkeley juries, especially in a political case.

Indeed, my life was threatened. My wife was told that I would be murdered. So I had no sympathy with the idea that these were idealistic, young people committed to the highest principles of non-violence. I knew it was total nonsense. Many of them were mentally ill, they had become unhinged by the FSM, they had aspirations that vastly exceeded the aspirations we set out in the FSM. This is why I've never been sympathetic with these revolutionary movements, like Castro's or Che Guevara's. I've always thought these were dreadful and monstrous people, and the people they want to kill are people like you and me.

> "The right is so stupid that it's not even worth discussing. But the left is evil."
>
> (From an interview published in the *Los Angeles Times*, December 28, 1999).

I never had any illusions about these people and I never had any illusions about the revolutionaries in Berkeley. I wanted free speech, but that was very much within the tradition of liberal, constitutional democracy. I did not want a Marxist revolution in this country and I didn't want a small Marxist revolution on this campus. And I did everything I could to fight against it.

And I succeeded. In two years, we had created the mechanisms whereby the University could function as an intellectual institution rather than as a political institution. It wasn't easy, but we did that. That meant that in 1968, when the rest of the world blew up, we had no serious problems in Berkeley. I went to Paris in the Spring of 68 and found it in an upheaval. Various places in England were also having upheavals. But by that time Berkeley was under control

G. F.:

So you did no philosophy at all during those three years.

John Searle:

No. But it was a difficult time in my life. It was very stressful for my wife who was then a law student. The whole thing was extremely difficult because we had two children, and I was first running a revolution, and then running a counterrevolution, and making a lot of enemies, having sleepless nights... it was a stressful period in my life.

G. F.:

You summarized that experience in your book *The Campus War*. That's the only one of your books that I wasn't able to buy a copy of.

John Searle:

The Campus War was politically incorrect. It came out at a time when people wanted to be told that this is the most wonderful generation of students in American history and they're doing all these wonderfully idealistic things. And it's a kind of miracle that they're so successful. And the miracle is that their idealism is overcoming the corruption and cynicism of the ruling classes.

My own view was quite different. I was interested in the question, "How could these people succeed, and what sorts of people were involved?" And I wrote a book that was not celebratory. It wasn't sympathetic to the right wing because I didn't say, "This is all a Communist plot run from Moscow and Cuba." That was nonsense. But I was not sympathetic to the student movement, certainly not to its more revolutionary aspirations. So the book was not popular. I think it was more popular in France and England. It also came out in a French translation.

G. F.:

I don't think there was a Spanish translation.

John Searle:

No, there was never a Spanish translation. Oddly enough, this is the one book that I wrote on a popular subject for a general audience and it's much less successful than all my technical books. Copies are scarce. My wife found one on the web the other day so she's going to order it from the bookstore. It's a collector's item.

Affirmative Action

G. F.:

Are you involved at all in University government right now?

John Searle:

No. I did make a speech on the Academic Senate recently, in which I criticized the Chancellor for yielding to student political pressure in making

63

an academic decision about the future of a department called Ethnic Studies, which was a department essentially founded for political reasons rather than for intellectual reasons. But that was an unusual case for me. I haven't been doing that recently. I did it because people asked me to do it.

G. F.:

That's related, I guess, to the affirmative action debate.

John Searle:

Right. Well, my attitude on affirmative action is this. There are different meanings of affirmative action. The original meaning was one I was sympathetic with. Namely, that the University and the society at large should take affirmative action to see that people who have not previously had a chance to compete for success in American life, are given extra encouragement to compete.

I am, myself, part Cherokee. So I am personally aware that a lot of groups in American society, like the Native Americans, the Blacks, and to some extent the Hispanics, have really been discouraged from participating in mainstream life in the country. And I wanted affirmative action to overcome that form of discrimination.

64

But the meaning of affirmative action was subtly changed. Affirmative action originally meant encouraging people to compete. But then it changed to mean criteria for judging the competition. So the idea was that if you had two people competing for a job, one a white male and the other a member of a so-called "targeted minority," such as a woman or a black person, even if the white male was superior, you would have to choose one of the others, assuming that they meet certain minimum criteria. You had to choose the inferior candidate.

I thought that was outrageous and I fought against it. I saw this in University employment. You have an opening for a job and you get applicants for this job. You narrow it down. You have a white male who is superior and then you have various members of minorities who are not as good. They meet minimal criteria - they have graduate degrees in philosophy and so on. You are required under affirmative action to hire the less qualified person and tell the best person, "We won't hire you because you're a white male." That's racial discrimination, and I fought against it.

G. F.:

I understand that, but some people claim that's maybe the only way to counterbalance the historical bias against certain minorities.

John Searle:

Well, they do say that. The common argument is that unless we do this, that is unless we cheat, the University will be insufficiently representative. My own view is that it's not the aim of the University to be representative. We are not a political institution in that way. Our aim is to be intellectually superior, and it might turn out that in order to be the best university in the world you have to have certain groups more represented than others. I mean, we're going to have more Jewish mathematicians than we're going to have black female mathematicians, simply because there's a tradition among the Jews in the United States of studying mathematics.

For example, I know people who do set theory in our University. They are white males, and a disproportionate number of them are Jews. Now, am I to say, "Well, we shouldn't hire these people because they're not black people?" No. They're the best in the world at what they do, and that's the sort of person we are trying to hire. However, my view is not universally accepted. A lot of people think, "No, we don't want to hire just the best people. We want to hire the people who will be more representative."

Another argument is that you need to hire people who are like your students so that your students will be inspired by these people; they'll be role models. And I was not very sympathetic to that. The people who were my role models were totally unlike me. They were tweedy Englishmen who had gone to snobbish public schools in England. They were people like Austin and Strawson.

G. F.:

This latter argument runs the risk of converting an argument *for* diversity into an argument *against* diversity: you need to have an identical role model in order to be inspired.

John Searle:

Exactly. And it's a kind of racism, because it says black people can't learn except from black people, women can't learn except from women. And I don't believe it. I don't think that's true.

This, by the way, is essential to our conception of higher education. We do not believe that you have to be a Marxist to teach Marx, or that you have to be a Wittgensteinean to teach Wittgenstein, or that you have to be a member of the Catholic faith to teach St. Thomas Aquinas. We think intelligent people can teach these subjects, and I think you do not have to be a black person to teach the history of black people in the United States. But this assumption has been quietly abandoned. In this University we have a Department of Women's Studies mostly run by feminist women. It is not essentially an academic intellectual department. It's a political action group.

"You don't build your life around being left-handed, and you don't build your life around your ethnicity or your race. These are just stupid accidents of your birth."

From John Searle Interview: Conversations with History; Institute of International Studies, UC Berkeley. (http://globetrotter.berkeley.edu/people/Searle/searle-con0.html)

G. F.:

What courses are you teaching now?

John Searle:

I teach undergraduates on The Philosophy of Mind and on The Philosophy of Language. I taught a graduate seminar last Spring and I'm teaching one this Spring. I teach one graduate course a year. This Spring I will teach a seminar on *free will*. Last year I taught one on *rationality*.

G. F.:

I wanted to ask you about your picture on the cover of Cambridge Press books, like *Speech Acts* or *Expression and Meaning*. That's not very common for a philosopher, to have his portrait on the cover of his books.

John Searle:

That was the idea of the editors; they proposed that we put that picture on. The picture was actually taken in Paris. I had given a lecture and a bunch of us went out after the lecture. It was my last lecture and I was feeling relaxed. It was a hot afternoon and we went to an outdoor cafe on Boulevard Montparnasse. Do you know where *La Coupole* is? The big restaurant? Across the street there's a bar called *Le Bar Select*, and we went to *Le Bar Select*. It's an outdoor cafe. It's not my favorite, but I like *La*

69

Coupole and I like the Boulevard Montparnasse and we ordered a glass of white wine and we drank it. Then we ordered some more glasses, and in the end we wished we had ordered bottles, as it would have been cheaper.

There was this nice woman, a German photographer named Anne Selders. Anne took these pictures and I liked one of them... here it is, here. I had a jacket and tie on, because I had been lecturing. It's been on the covers of books ever since.

Philosophy of Mind

Where is cognitive science going?

G. F.:

How do you see the field of cognitive science today? Where is it going? What's your assessment?

John Searle:

As you know, originally, cognitive science was founded on a mistake. It was founded on the mistake of supposing that the brain is a digital computer and the mind is a computer program. I've never believed that. The view that mental states could be defined in terms of their causal relations to input-stimuli, to other mental states, and to output-behavior, was an extension of functionalism in the philosophy of mind.

*functional-
ism*

I think that now the computational model of the mind in cognitive science is gradually fading out, and is being replaced by something I welcome, namely cognitive neuroscience. I think we're now beginning, with the invention of fMRI (functional

71

magnetic resonance imaging) techniques and other techniques, to get an understanding of the brain and how it functions in cognition, which we've never been able to understand before.

So, I think cognitive science is more exciting than ever, but that's because it failed. The original project failed. The project of a computational science of cognition was bound to fail. But we are making progress with brain science.

G. F.:

Is there any positive content left to be rescued from that failure?

John Searle:

Sure. First of all, cognitive science overcame "behaviorism," which had been the orthodoxy in psychology.

> "And the science of psychology on the behaviorist model was you were going to correlate these stimulus inputs with the behavioral outputs. It's a ridiculous conception of the mind-- the idea is that there's nothing going on in there, except you have the stimulus input and the behavioral output.
>
> The best comment about behaviorism is the old joke about the two behaviorists after they just had sex. He says to

her, "It was great for you, how was it for me?" If behaviorism were right, that ought to make perfectly good sense, because there's nothing going on in him except his behavior, and she's in a better position to observe his behavior than he is."

From *Reason magazine* - February 2000. Reality Principles: An Interview with John R. Searle. By Edward Feser and Steven Postrel.

Also, in the early days I made a distinction between strong A.I. and weak A.I. Strong A.I. is the view that the appropriately programmed digital computer literally has a mind because that's all there is to having a mind. I refuted that, or I think I did. And the other view I call weak A.I. That is the view that you can use the computer to study the mind as you can use it to study anything. And we have a lot of useful computational studies of cognitive processes. You can do useful computational simulations and models of cognitive processes as you can do computational simulations of economic processes. It's a useful tool.

G. F.:

If you are right about the importance of these breakthroughs in neurophysiology, and we eventually come to know how the brain really works, does that mean that scholars who work on the philosophy of mind will become unemployed?

73

John Searle:

In fact, changes that are now going on in cognitive science make the philosophy of mind more interesting. Cognitive science was founded on the mistake that the brain is a digital computer and the mind is a computer program. It's not the first time in history that a science was founded on a mistake. Chemistry was founded on alchemy, and cultural anthropology was founded on the false idea that people are infinitely malleable and variable. I don't think that this mistake is fatal, but I do think that we are now moving into a new paradigm, away from computational cognitive science, to cognitive neuroscience. And I welcome that.

Now we are investigating how the brain functions. And as we find out more about how the brain functions, we're going to have a much more rigorous cognitive science. That seems to me not to put an end to philosophical discussion, but to create all sorts of philosophical problems that we didn't have before. For example, I've just published an article in the *Annual Review of Neuroscience,* where I claim that a lot of the neuroscientific research is based on a false premise. It's based on the premise that in order to understand how the brain causes consciousness, we should try to find out how it causes a single building-block of consciousness, such as the experience of red or a certain kind of sound. And I argue that the subject can only experience red if he or she is already conscious. He can only hear a sound if he's already conscious. So I oppose what I call a *building-block theory* to the *unified field theory*. And I make a claim that the unified field of consciousness is what we should be investigating. And to investigate that, we have to investigate what's the difference between the conscious brain and the unconscious brain.

I give that as one example, but I see philosophical investigation as really an important part of cognitive neuroscience. Let me give you some other examples. One of the scandalous notions in the philosophy of mind today, really an outrageous scandal, is that we don't have a coherent account of the unconscious. People talk glibly about unconscious mental states, but I don't think they know what they're talking about. And the idea that many of us have is that an unconscious mental state is just like a conscious mental state only minus the consciousness. But it isn't clear what that means. I don't think we can get on without the notion of the unconscious, but I think it needs a lot more clarification. So I don't see that brain science is going to put an end to the philosophy of mind. On the contrary, I see it as opening up a whole new area of investigation.

The Chinese Room

"I imagine that I'm locked in a room with a lot of Chinese symbols (that's the database) and I've got a rule book for shuffling the symbols (that's the program) and I get Chinese symbols put in the room through a slit, and those are questions put to me in Chinese. And then I look up in the rule book what I'm supposed to do with these symbols and then I give them back symbols and unknown to me, the stuff that comes in are questions and the stuff I give back are answers.

Now, if you imagine that the programmers get good at writing the rule book and I get good at shuffling the symbols, my answers are fine. They look like answers of a native Chinese [speaker]. They ask me questions in Chinese, I answer the questions in Chinese. All the same, I don't understand a word of Chinese. And the bottom line is, if I don't understand Chinese on the basis of implementing the computer program for understanding Chinese, then neither does any other digital computer on that basis, because no computer's got anything that I don't have. That's the power of the computer, it just shuffles symbols. It just manipulates symbols. So I am a computer for understanding Chinese, but I don't understand a word of Chinese.

You can see this point if you contrast Searle in Chinese with Searle in English. If they ask me questions in English and I give answers back in English, then my answers will be as good as a native English speaker, because I am one. And if they gave me questions in Chinese and I give them back answers in Chinese, my answers will be as good as a native Chinese speaker because I'm running the Chinese program. But there's a huge difference on the inside. On the outside it looks the same. On the inside I understand English and I don't understand Chinese. In English I am a human being who understands English; in Chinese I'm just a computer. Computers, therefore -- and this really is the decisive point -- just in virtue of implementing a program, the computer is not guaranteed understanding. It might have understanding for some other reason but just going through the steps of the formal program is not sufficient for the mind."

From John Searle Interview: Conversations with History; Institute of International Studies, UC Berkeley. (http://globetrotter.berkeley.edu/people/Searle/searle-con0.html)

G. F.:

After twenty years of debate on the *Chinese Room* argument: do you feel there was any progress, or that people always went back to the same issues?

John Searle:

Well, both. The way *The Chinese Room* argument evolved is sort of funny. In the early days of cognitive science, there was a foundation called the Sloan Foundation that funded people to go around the country and lecture. We were facetiously called "Sloan Rangers". I was invited to go to Yale to lecture in the Artificial Intelligence Lab. I knew nothing about artificial intelligence. I bought a book to read on the airplane, written by Roger Schank and Robert Abelson, who were at the A.I. lab. I read it on the plane and they talked about these story-understanding programs. And I thought, well, that's ridiculous. There's an easy refutation. Let the story be in Chinese and let me be the computer. I still won't understand the story. That's the origin of the Chinese Room Argument.

It is amazing how hard it is to get people to see what the argument is. It's a very simple argument. But people are so much in the grip of a bunch of traditional categories that they literally cannot grasp the argument. They think that I'm arguing that a machine can't think whereas, in my view, the brain *is* a machine. And they think I'm arguing that you couldn't build an artifact, an artificial machine that could think whereas, in my view, building an artificial brain is in principle like building an artificial heart. It's just a question of finding out how the heart works and doing it, then finding out how the brain works and doing it. So that was never the point. People can't get that. They think I'm trying to refute the idea that machines can think, and they think that somehow I think there's some magical quality about biology, that only a biological system like the brain can think.

It's amazing to me. I explicitly rejected both of those mistakes in the original article. I said, "The brain is a machine," and "of course, you can build, in principle, an artifact that did what the brain does. You have to replicate the causal powers." And I think it is partly because they're in the grip of all these traditional categories of mind, body, man, machine, and so on, that they misunderstand my argument.

They don't understand how computers work. They think that a computer is essentially made of silicon and that it does information processing the way car engines are essentially made of metal and do internal combustion. But they're totally different. You see there's a paradox. The problem with the digital computer is not that it's too much of a machine to think, but that it's not enough of a machine. Even though the computing machine you buy in a store is a machine, the computational processes are not intrinsically machine processes. They are abstract, algorithmic, mathematical processes that we have found ways to implement on a machine. And that's a very hard idea for people to get.

Gustavo Faigenbaum

I don't have any doubts that my argument is going to win. In the long run, the argument is based on two logical principles that are unassailable. One is that the *syntax* or the symbols of the computer implementation are not by themselves *semantics*. They're not enough to constitute semantic content. And secondly, *simulation* is not *duplication*. Those are two rock bottom logical points and that's why the argument will succeed.

But there is another thing that I didn't anticipate. In philosophy we just assume everybody's going to try to refute us and in fifty years the original thought will be found to be mistaken. But these guys think they're doing something called Science, with a capital "S". And it's almost like a religion. They think unless the brain is a digital computer, we're forced to some kind of mysticism and we're out of business and we'll lose our research grants. So there is a personal commitment to the computational model, which I had never seen before.

I mean, Catholics are not nearly so passionate about the soul as strong A.I. people are about the mind as a program. I don't have any problems presenting my views to the Catholics. I lectured in the Vatican. The Pope invited me. This was last summer, and I met the Pope. And they didn't seem to be too shocked by my views. "We've got this guy

80

who obviously doesn't agree with us, but here are his views." Whereas, the strong A.I. people are passionately opposed to the *Chinese Room*. They have a fit every time they think about the *Chinese Room*.

There's going to be a volume called *The Twentieth Anniversary of the Chinese Room*. It's not out yet. I have written an article for that book called *Twenty Years in the Chinese Room* where I make some of the points I just made.

G. F.:

One of the cognitive science professors at the university where I work, Ricardo Minervino, told me that the argument works better with non-experts than with experts. When he is teaching the *Chinese Room* to his students they are all convinced by it. But then, probably someone who is a defender of A.I. wouldn't see anything final about it. So, Ricardo was asking me, "Does that speak well, or badly, of the argument?"

John Searle:

Two things are clear. One is that professionals have commitments. If you have an argument for the non-existence of God, it is not going to go over well with Jesuits, for all kinds of personal reasons. But

81

Gustavo Faigenbaum

there is something else. Intuitively, the experts are used to thinking in terms of systems, and their immediate response on hearing the argument is to make the systems reply. To say, "Well, it's the whole room, and you're just the central processing unit. And, of course, it's the whole system that thinks." Now that won't work for reasons I've explained. Namely, if I don't understand because I don't know the meanings of any words, then neither does the room because the room's got no way of figuring out the meanings of the words any more than I do.

The professionals usually think, "Well, we have an answer to this." It's not a good answer, but they do have something they can say. Whereas, ordinary people say, "I don't understand Chinese, obviously." Do you understand these points? There are two features that professionals have. One is a deep personal commitment - they can't give up, they'd have to give up their life work in many cases if they're strong A.I. people. But secondly, they're used to thinking in terms of systems and ordinary people don't.

G. F.:

Now, if someone is doing specific cognitive science research, for instance on computerized models of analogy, does the argument have complete implications for the way a researcher conducts her project?

John Searle:

No. That sounds like weak A.I. to me. One concrete implication would be this: in designing robots, the temptation is to think the way to get the robot to behave like a human is to put in digital computer programs. However, scientists' efforts to build human-like robots by means of digital computer programming seemed to produce crude simpletons. The only exceptions are things like Deep Blue, where you get enormous computational power, but where you're no longer trying to do A.I. at all. You're not trying to imitate humans on processing levels.

G. F.:

Deep Blue had a huge database.

John Searle:

Yes, and a huge computational power. In a way, Deep Blue is giving up on A.I. because it doesn't say, "Well we're going to try to do what human beings do," but it says "We're just going to overpower them with brute force. Calculate two

83

hundred million moves per second and we are going to do it."

Information processing

John Searle:

There is something, though, that I'm not completely satisfied about my own views. We need to think very seriously about the notion of *information*, and *information processing*. I argue in various places that it's a mistake to think that the unconscious level of information processing that goes on the brain is *literally* information processing. That's a metaphorical attribution to the steps the brain goes through, and whereby it produces intrinsic information in the form of thoughts and perceptions in the agent. But in the stages in between, though they impact in such a way as to cause for example a conscious perception, there's literally no information. There is just a sequence of causes and effects.

I think that's right, but I think we need to say some more about it. I mean, why is it that the information processing terminology is so useful to us? Why does it seem to be so functional and so important when you're describing how the brain is able to produce a visual experience, for example?

Now, the visual experience, in my view, has intrinsic information because it's got intentionality. It has intentional content. But the actual sequence of neurological events that lead from the retina to the visual experience doesn't have any information. Those events are just blind processes that we can describe *as if* they had some mental content or intentional content. But they're not literally that way. However, I think we need to know more. The fact is that the information processing terminology is very useful.

G. F.:

In developmental cognitive psychology, information processing is a very basic assumption. Yet it is not clear for me whether cognitive psychologists are referring to a neurophysiological, hard-wired process, or to an intermediate level of information processing, between the level of neurophysiology and the level of conscious, intentional experience.

John Searle:

Well, originally cognitive science was based on the assumption that there was an intermediate level between the level of common sense intentionality and the level of neurobiology. And that was the level of the computer program. Now that's false. I think I

85

refuted that view. There is no such level. However, the fact remains that it is useful to describe a lot of the processes that go on at the neurobiological level as if they were *thinking*, as if they were doing information processing. Now I say that you need to distinguish between those features of the world that exist only relative to us, the observer-relative, and the observer-independent features.

Now if the book is on the table, and I see the book is on the table, that's observer independent. It doesn't matter what other people think. But when people say that information about the book was already present in the lateral geniculate nucleus, that's observer relative. They're saying there's some neuron firing in the lateral geniculate nucleus, which later on produces such and such information in the experience. I think that's a harmless way of speaking provided you don't think that there's literally some intentionality going on at this lower level. There isn't. Most people in cognitive science just don't get it. They don't understand what I'm talking about. They think it's obvious there is information there. Don't you see? The guy gets photons on a retina and later on he sees a book. There must be some information in between. It doesn't follow, of course, but it's very hard to get people to see that it doesn't.

G. F.:

Therefore, your argument basically consists in a conceptual distinction.

John Searle:

Yes. If you're going to do science, you have to understand the distinction between the features of reality that are observer independent and those that are observer relative. You can't begin to do science without that.

G. F.:

But then, why is it useful at all to think of the brain as processing information?

John Searle:

Well, because you want to know how a series of stimuli on the retina can cause an actual conscious experience, which is rich with information. And you want to know how the elements of the stimulus produced that information in the actual experience. And there really is information in the experience. And then it's almost irresistible to think, "Well, really, it's kind of like a telephone wire. I mean, the information was there all along. It's just that we need to decode it."

87

Now that's wrong. I'm sure that's the wrong way to think of it. But what is exactly the right way to describe it? I don't know. And I think it's useful at this stage of the research to be able to describe how such and such a neuron firing, or such and such neuro-biological pattern, later on causes information in the actual experience. And it's irresistible to think, "Well, in some sense that information must have been present."

Marr is the worst offender here. It's almost regarded as bad taste to criticize Marr because he's such a saintly figure, you know, he died very young. But Marr's computational theory of vision used information processing in the way I am criticizing.

G. F.:

Yet, I tend to think that there must be some essential difference between the process of digestion – to use your own example – and thinking. Even though both are biological processes, there must be something more in thinking, which maybe could be explained in terms of this analogy with information processes.

John Searle:

88

You see, here is the way I think of it. There's a series of blind, brute neurobiological processes, and they cause a visual experience. It's useful sometimes to think of those processes as bearing information because, of course, the information that is in the visual experience has to get there somehow, and it has to be derived from the impact of the photons on the retina. But you shouldn't suppose that there is any intrinsic information in there. In the stomach you have a lot of brute, blind, gastronomical processes that cause digestion. And often it's useful to think of those in terms of information. Of course we're not tempted to think, "Well, there must be information in there really." You know, that's just a metaphor. Now we think there must be information in the brain, in this literal sense, because it's very hard for us to grasp that you can have a meaningful input and a meaningful output, and that all the processes in between are meaningless.

Connectionism

John Searle:

This is why connectionism was a useful stage in this development: it made it clear that the intervening processes are meaningless. There's no point in the connectionist network where you can say, "Well, this is where it is making an inference, or where it represents truths, etc." It's just a series of vectors. And I think that's closer to how the brain works.

G. F.:

So, is this neurobiological approach to cognitive science overcoming not only the digital computer model, but also the connectionist network model?

John Searle:

Yes, I think so. However, we're not overcoming the information metaphor because people still talk that way. And we have to respect this. There must be something very useful about this talk. They still talk as if there was all this information going on in the brain. But we need to distinguish between the level of real information, where you have a thought process or some other intrinsic mental state, and the *as-if* or observer-relative talk of "information," which is just a useful manner of speaking.

Cognitive Psychology and the Theory Theory

G. F.:

Would your criticisms also apply to nativist psychology? Cognitive developmental psychologists talk about infants having innate theoretical principles that somehow constrain their development of naïve physics.

John Searle:

You see, it's very important to distinguish genuine cases of rule following from behavior which is rule described, where you can describe the behavior according to certain general principles. I mean, take a case where it's obvious. In the case of vision, I cannot see infrared or ultraviolet. But that's not because I'm following the rule: If it's infrared, don't see it, or if it's ultraviolet, don't see it. That's just how the visual system is made. There's a principle on which the visual system is made, namely it's sensitive to certain parts of the color spectrum and not to other parts. Now I want to say exactly the same is true for things like language acquisition. When the child acquires a language, there are certain languages he can acquire and certain languages he can't, but it doesn't follow from that, that he's following a rule.

G. F.:

Intentionality is absent, because the normative aspect of rule following, as well as the sense of obligation, is absent too.

John Searle:

That's right. If there is no normative aspect, if it's absolutely automatic, if it's not voluntary, if it's not subject to interpretation, and it's not accessible to consciousness, then it looks like you don't have rule following. It looks like you just got rule described behavior. If I fall off a building, I will fall according to the rule that $S=1/2\ GT^2$. But I'm not following that rule as I go toward the ground. I'm not thinking, "Well I better speed up or slow down otherwise," because I can't. It's just automatic. And it may be that that's how the brain works. Certainly that's how the visual system works.

And, of course, there is a homunculi fallacy too. It is almost irresistible to think there must be some homunculus in the kid that tells her which rules to follow.

G. F.:

So what about children's *theories of mind*?

John Searle:

Well, I'm very reluctant to call it a theory. I think Alison Gopnik calls it a theory.

G. F.:

Oh, sure, among many other authors in contemporary cognitive psychology, like Janet Astington, Michael Chandler, Annette Karmiloff-Smith, Joseph Perner, etc.

John Searle:

I haven't read the literature on this, but I'm very suspicious of the idea that the child acquires a theory. I think it's more likely that the child acquires a set of skills.

G. F.:

What many "Theory of Mind" theorists say is that when the child explains other people's behavior she has to postulate that they have feelings, beliefs, and desires. So, children have a complex conceptual

93

apparatus that allows them to explain and interpret other people's behavior. And children's ontological and theoretical commitments undergo change, and sometimes such change might result from attempts to deal with empirical evidence. So, for instance, they postulate that the child moves on from a desire-psychology to a desire-and-beliefs-psychology. Now they compare this theory-forming activity in the child with theory-development in science.

John Searle:

Do they say this for animals too?

G. F.:

No.

John Searle:

Why not?

G. F.:

Well, I think they would say that a dog, for instance, would remain at the first stage, at a "desire-psychology" stage. I think so. There are some controversies about whether apes can deceive, whether they can manipulate other people's beliefs, and therefore whether they can be said to have a theory of mind.

John Searle:

You see, I was struck by the fact that when my dog, Ludwig, was a small puppy, he would chew everything, but he would not bite hard on my hand. He would take my hand in his mouth and he would bite a little bit, but wouldn't chew my arm off the way he would chew on bones and sticks and so on. And why not? Well, I think he probably is just predisposed to behave toward other living beings in a way that is different from the way that he behaves toward the natural world. But you could say, he has a theory that you're a sentient being, and that you're conscious.

G. F.:

Yes, or at least some of them would say that there is some theoretical principle, or a core theoretical domain underlying your dog's behavior.

John Searle:

I want to know what is involved in the notion that it's a theory as opposed to a skill. When I bounce a ball off a wall, Ludwig knows where to go to catch it. But that's not because he has a theory of physics.

95

He doesn't have a theory that says "go to the point where the plane of the angle of incidence equals the angle of reflection in a parabolic arc, the flatness of whose trajectory is a function of impact velocity minus friction". That's a theory. And if I were building a robot that would do this, I would put this theory in because we don't have a better technology. But I think it's misleading to say that Ludwig has that theory. I think he just has a skill. And this is not just a terminological point. Now they might refute me by some empirical evidence, but the evidence I've seen suggests the idea that what Ludwig has is a skill. And what the child acquires is a set of skills or of abilities for coping. That is what I call *the Background*.

However, I want to say at some level this is still an open empirical question. We've got to know more about what goes on in the child's brain. The stuff I've seen so far is not conclusive for the theory theory. It is just as good evidence for the skill theory.

Most people don't get the idea that you might account for all this in term of skills. I don't think they get the concept of the Background. And the reason is, in our intellectual tradition we over-intellectualized the mind. We think everything the mind does must be the application of rules and principles. This goes back to Descartes.

96

G. F.:

Would you say then that the judge for this debate is empirical research on the neurobiological level?

John Searle:

Yes.

G. F.:

What about just studying the process of conceptual development?

John Searle:

You might. That might settle it too. But you want to be sure that you've got a test that will distinguish between just having a skill and having a theory. Because Ludwig might pass their test for having a theory, it's just he doesn't have a theory. He has a skill.

Gustavo Faigenbaum

Reductionism

G. F.:

What about hermeneutic or narrative approaches to the mind or to psychology? My impression is that you don't see that as a valid scientific approach.

John Searle:

I'm not sure whom you have in mind, but most of the hermeneutics I've seen is pretty superficial. Of course, when we're doing literary studies, we have to have interpretive methods. And when we're doing studies of what I call *the Background*, it seems to me there are narrative structures in the Background. So we have a certain set of expectations of what it is to go into a restaurant and eat a meal, or what it is to fall in love, or what it is to get a job, or what it is to travel to South America. And those influence our behavior. But I don't see the narrative approach as a rival to a scientific cognitive science. I think they complement each other.

G. F.:

So would you say that it makes sense to study conceptual, affective, or social processes without the horizon of an eventual reduction to neuropsychology?

John Searle:

Well, you know, the notion of reduction is tricky. Of course all psychology has to be going on in the brain, but if reduction means there's no real level of psychology I think that's wrong. There is a real level. I mean there is a real level of conscious and intentional rule following, and rational decision-making. Now, it's questionable to what extent that presupposes free will. And I talk about that in my new book, which is about rationality. I think it does presuppose free will. It presupposes that where certain conscious processes are concerned, the brain states are not causally sufficient for the next state. That consciousness is essential. And that's a difficult point.

Of course we want a scientific account that explains the behavior of big things in terms of little things. That has been the history of science for the past 350 years and it's immensely successful. If you want to understand matter, look at atoms. If you

Gustavo Faigenbaum

want to understand diseases, look at microorganisms. To understand genetics, look at the DNA molecule. And we want to know how that works in the brain. Is the basic level that of the neuron? Is it the synapse? We need to investigate all that. But there is a temptation to think that that kind of reduction is a form of eliminative reduction and that's what I reject. You can do a *causal* reduction of the mind to the brain, but you can't do an *eliminative* reduction of anything that actually exists. And the mind actually exists, these mental states actually exist.

G. F.:

In *Minds, Brains and Science* you claim that the right kind of explanation for mental processes, indeed the only explanation we can reasonably expect from science, is an account of neurobiological processes. If we had a detailed knowledge of neurobiology at the microlevel, we should be able to predict the resulting mental phenomena. Certain basic neuropsychological facts would cause certain mental experiences, such as the experience of "pain". Is it possible that even a very simple sensation, like for example a pinch in the hand, be subjective in the sense of being perceived differently by each person? If that were the case, then we would not be able to predict a

100

mental experience from a given neurobiological pattern.

John Searle:

Well, if you've got a phenomenologically simple thing like pain, then it seems likely that, if the neurobiological causes of your pain and the causes of my pain are similar enough, then the pains will be similar in experience. That is, if the neurobiology of pain is shared between different people, then to the extent that you get an identity of neurobiology, you get an identity of pain. But what's more interesting is where you get more complex things. Maybe you have different kinds of anxiety, or maybe your way of falling in love is different from my way of falling in love. You may get quite striking individual differences. This is the old red/green problem, how do I know you don't have the experience I would call seeing red when you have the experience you call seeing green? But the answer to that is that we know enough about your neurobiology to know that the rods and the cones, etc. are the same. We know that you have the same kind of neurobiological structures that underlie visual experiences.

Free Will

G. F.:

Now, the question is, does the relationship between the microlevel and the higher levels presuppose a deterministic model of physical causality? And, is that model still acceptable for contemporary science?

John Searle:

Well, you've asked the most difficult question. And I now think that the chapter I wrote in *Minds, Brains and Science*, contains a mistake or at least I wouldn't do it that way today. I've just written a book on rationality and I argue that if free will is a real fact, then it must be a fact about how the brain works. And I then describe two alternative hypotheses to account for free choice. One is the hypothesis that the underlying neurological structures are at every point causally sufficient to produce the next state, even though our experience is one of freedom. Now, if that's right, then free will is an illusion, because all of out actions are determined in advance. But there's another hypothesis, and that is that consciousness in the brain is a system feature. And though the behavior

102

of the microelements at any point will be sufficient to determine whether or not the brain is conscious, and what its conscious contents are, the conscious contents, which are a system feature, may well determine the next state of the brain in a way that is not based on causally sufficient conditions.

So, in this second view, consciousness is a system feature. And we know that it's possible to think about the universe in a non-deterministic way from quantum mechanics. And here's a possible way of thinking about free will. The brain is a conscious system, and the consciousness of the brain at any given point, though it's entirely fixed by the behavior of microelements, that consciousness together with it the microelements, are not causally sufficient to fix the next state of the system. And, indeed, what fixes the next state of the system is a conscious decision. And the conscious decision is, of course, realized in the microstructure. So we don't get any kind of dualism. There is no dualism of mind and body. The lack of causally sufficient conditions at the system level goes all the way down.

Now I'm very suspicious of all the quantum mechanics talk in brain science. People think quantum mechanics is going to be the magical solution. But I do think this much - quantum mechanics has taught us one thing: it is possible to think about the most fundamental features of the universe in non-deterministic fashion. Now, if so, then it's an empirical hypothesis and an empirical question whether or not the brain is a completely deterministic system. And if free will is real, if we really do have free will, then the brain cannot be a completely deterministic system. And what would be the level at which it's non-deterministic? It would be the level at which the conscious brain is capable of making free decisions on the basis of rational considerations, but not on the basis of causally sufficient antecedent conditions.

I have a chapter in my new book (on rationality) where I discuss this - the chapter on free will - the last chapter in the book. I don't know if that's right, but I do think that it's at least an empirical possibility that brain science that might find out that we do have a genuine free will and not just the illusion of free will. Now, I haven't read *Minds, Brains and Science* in a long time, but the way I remember it, I thought that if the bottom-up causation was sufficient to fix the complete state of consciousness at every point in conscious life, that would be sufficient for determinism. But, of course, it isn't, because determinism is not a thesis about the relationship of the micro and the macro in any given point in time. It's a thesis about the behavior of the whole system across time. And it might well be that at any given point in time you have a complete bottom-up determination of the conscious state of the system, even though the conscious state of the system can then lead to the next state of the system without antecedently sufficient causal conditions. Now if you understand all that, then you understand more than most professionals. But, anyway, that's what I put in my latest book.

I think, you see, either evolution has given us genuine free will or it hasn't. If it hasn't, then it's the biggest illusion in history. Then we have this huge, elaborate, biologically expensive capacity of the brain for conscious decision making which is a total illusion. All of our bodily movements are determined in advance by the plumbing in the brain and conscious decision-making makes no difference at all to our behavior. That's one hypothesis.

G. F.:

The foam on the wave.

John Searle:

The foam on the wave, epiphenomenalism. Or, another hypothesis is, no, it's real. We really do have the capacity for free choice. But, as a neurobiological thesis then, that is the thesis that at any given point in the decision making process, the brain's state, though sufficient to fix consciousness at that point, is not sufficient to fix the next state of the system.

Mind and Culture

G. F.:

Animals or babies have emotions, beliefs, and desires. But you point out that we also have specific types of desires like envy or rage or lust. Not only do we have beliefs, but we also have hunches, or we feel certain about something. Now, are such varieties also grounded on biology? To what extent do those distinctions depend on social or linguistic codifications? Could we possibly have a hunch without having the linguistic category of "a hunch"?

John Searle:

I think that is a very good question. The basic attitudes and emotions are built into our biological structure. But in order to get the refinement of distinctions, as well as a certain refinement of content, you need language, and you need a certain kind of culture. My favorite quotation is from *Le Duc* La Rochefoucauld, 18th century French essayist and philosopher; he wrote this sort of maxims. He says, "Very few people would ever fall in love if they never read about it." That's one of his best.

106

What he's driving at is that you need a certain kind of dramatic scenario in order to fall in love. I mean, Ludwig has passionate desires for female dogs, but he doesn't fall in love. And for our conception of falling in love, as something more than just sexual desire, you've got to have a language; you have to have a special set of linguistic categories

G. F.:

And the Greeks fell in love in a different way.

John Searle:

A different way. That's right. Yeah.

G. F.:

There is a German author called Albrecht Dihle, who says that the Greeks didn't actually have the concept of the will. They had *proairesis*, which might be translated as "deliberate decision;" and *boule*, which is like "wanting to do something." But the concept of *voluntas* is specifically a Roman-Latin concept, first worked out by Augustine and there's nothing similar to that in the Greeks.

John Searle:

107

My colleague, Alan Code, says that we misunderstand Aristotle. That when we think that Aristotle thought that you could only deliberate about the means and not about the ends, that is based on mistranslations. He had a different concept of rationality and of mind altogether. And I think it's not at all easy to understand historical figures. Just to put it in very simple terms, a lot of people think that it would be wonderful to live in ancient Athens, but if they actually found themselves in such a place they would be disgusted. I mean: the smell, the plumbing, the filth.

G. F.:

And you better be a citizen.

John Searle:

That's right. They always imagine somehow they're going to be in the upper class and not going to be a slave. And the same with people who admire the Middle Ages. I think that a person with our background couldn't possibly find life agreeable in the Middle Ages. It was filthy, disgusting, diseased and impoverished. But people have these fantasies about other cultures or about other phases in our own history. I think it's very difficult to understand historical figures and I'm sure that if my living contemporaries cannot understand my views, and I'm not a very difficult author, I think they would really have a hard time when it comes to Plato and Aristotle. They are probably having all kinds of systematic misunderstandings.

G. F.:

But do you think it is possible that such a basic concept like the will evolved historically, or that the Greeks already had a sense of the will?

John Searle:

I think that what happens is you get different ways that cultures have of representing a basic biological phenomenon. The basic phenomenon of voluntary action, the capacity to engage in voluntary action as opposed to say just digestion, that seems to me a basic fact of animal and human biology. My dog has that. He has the capacity for voluntary action. Now if you get theories about it, about freedom of the will and about certain things in the expression of the will, and about the actions of the will as an expression of character, those will vary from one culture to another. And it might well turn out that the Greeks had a different conception than we do. The underlying biology is the same. The theoretical superstructure will vary from culture to culture. See, in this day and age we were

109

confronted by that question at the time of the Gulf War: What was Saddam Hussein thinking? What were his friends thinking? And the answer is, they were thinking Allah will decide. You see, they have a kind of fatalism that's unintelligible to us. We think we're responsible. You better make the responsible decision. And they think it's in the hands of Allah. We don't think that way. Even our religious people don't think that way.

G. F.:

So now one starts getting the picture of the interactions between basic biological capacities and cultural narratives.

John Searle:

That's right.

Are meanings in the head? Internalism vs. externalism.

G. F.:

According to you, the content of a perceptual experience, let's say, someone dimly glimpses a man at a distance that is wearing a red cap, can be verbally expressed as follows: "There is a man there causing this visual experience and that man is wearing a red cap." You claim that perceptual realism is compatible with internalism. Now, isn't there a contradiction between your conception of intentionality as directed towards the world, and your claim that representations are internal?

John Searle:

I don't think there is. The idea is that I have a mental representation in the form of visual experience. This visual experience is directed at objects in the world, because it has the mind-to-world direction of fit. It's satisfied if, and only if, (1) there's a man there in a red hat and (2) the fact that there's a man there in a red hat is causing this visual experience. I don't see any problem with directionality.

It all depends on what you mean by directionality. If it's just direction of fit, then the direction is: from the mind to the world. The subject's mental representation in the form of a visual experience is supposed to give information about the world. And I'm reluctant to call those representations, because that suggests a kind of remoteness when, of course, I think it's more immediate: There is an immediate impact of the world on you when you see something. But the direction of causation – that's from the world to you.

— direction of causation – world to mind
— direction of fit – mind to world

Gustavo Faigenbaum

The world causes you to have the visual experience and, when you get the visual experience, you know how things are in the world. So, direction of fit is from mind to world, direction of causation is from world to mind. So far, I don't see any problem with internalism. Internalism just means that the intentional content is internal to my mental states. And I think that's right. I think that's how it works.

G. F.:

What is exactly at stake in the controversy about whether meanings are in the head or not in the head?

John Searle:

Well, a whole lot of things are at stake. One is the model. We need a model of how the mind works, and the traditional view which I think is right is that the contents of the mind are in the brain, and the contents of the mind are sufficient to determine how we relate to the real world when we think about it or when we refer to it. The externalists claim they've shown that to be false, but I think they are wrong.

What they have shown is that you need a richer conception of what's in the head. But what they have not shown is that somehow or other what is in

112

the head is insufficient to determine reference. Putnam says, "The world takes over," but of course the world always takes over on anybody's view because what the mind does is to set conditions, and then you refer to an object in the world if it satisfies those conditions. And what they've said is that conditions can't just be stated as just a bunch of general terms, but have to involve causal components as well.

So this is an important issue and I think they did make a valuable contribution in criticizing the traditional Aristotelian conception of concepts as a sort of checklist of features, e.g. "Man is a rational animal", "A horse is an equine quadruped". That won't do. You need to have conditions that will enable you to be in a causal contact with the world. That seems to be right.

The classical theory affirmed that the meaning of a word must be a sort of general checklist of general features, that you couldn't have these words defined indexically. And that's not true. I think that externalists are right about that. The classical theory was wrong in supposing that the meaning of a word is exhaustively given by a set of features, by a checklist of general features in the mind of the user of the word. And I'm sure that's a mistake for a lot of words.

But they misdescribe that when they say, "Well, that shows then that meanings are not in head." That doesn't follow. They assume that the meaning of a word is not in the mind of the agent. And that's not true. Putnam, in particular, thinks if it's an indexical definition, then it can't be internal to the mind. But it can be. "Water" is anything similar to this indexically presented stuff. That is to say water is anything identical in structure to the stuff that is now causing this visual experience. That's an entirely internal definition.

What is in the head is sufficient to determine reference, to determine how language relates to reality. And it has to be, otherwise we couldn't do it. We wouldn't know what we were talking about.

You get certain absurd results from externalism and, by and large, they have tried to pretend that those results are not absurd, and when they get absurdities, they tend to pretend that they're not absurdities. So, for example, one absurdity is that skepticism becomes logically impossible. If I were a brain in a vat, and all my beliefs would be caused by the fact that I am a brain in a vat, it follows on the externalist view that I must believe that I am a brain in a vat. If I'm a brain in a vat, then I believe that I'm a brain in a vat. There's no way I couldn't believe it since the content of my belief is caused by my causal situation, and my causal situation is that I'm

114

a brain in a vat. But, of course, the whole point of the brain in the vat fantasy is that I could have exactly the beliefs I have now, and still be a brain in a vat. What the externalist is saying is that we wouldn't have these beliefs. You'd really believe you are a brain in a vat. Thus, it's kind of a *reductio ad absurdum* of externalism.

They say this refutes skepticism. They say this shows that we cannot be meaningfully skeptical because if we skeptically doubted that we were brains in vats then our beliefs would be that we are brains in vats. The problem is, it doesn't seem that way to me. If I'm a brain in a vat, now it seems to me I'm sitting in a room in Berkeley, California, having a talk with Gustavo Faigenbaum. And I'm not a brain in a vat. But when I say those words, according to the externalist, the only way we can interpret those is, they mean I'm a brain in a vat, which is crazy.

G. F.:

The externalists constitute the canonical view of reference in contemporary philosophy.

John Searle:

Oh, yeah. Absolutely. The prevailing orthodoxy is externalism, and there are a very large number of

Ph.D. theses and other research proposals that are trying to work out the exact nature of the external relations that will determine both intentional content and thereby reference. These will all fail. We know in advance they will fail because they're based on a false premise.

G. F.:

And why is that? Why are externalists so strong today?

John Searle:

I don't know. But that's a good question. Partly, it's something new. It gives people a new paradigm. They got sick of working out the details of the Fregean account and here's something new to do. You can write Ph.D. theses, and you can do articles and books. The fact is nobody is getting anywhere. Nobody's ever giving a plausible account of this causal chain that's supposed to give content, and is entirely specifiable in third person terms. It's all supposed to be in neutral third person terms.

It's fascinating to see how after twenty years of externalism nobody has given a coherent account of what the external causal relations are supposed to be, except in internalist terms. And that you can do. But that's not what they want. They want an

116

account that makes no reference to the mind of the speaker; they want an account of how the causal chain connecting him to an object enables his utterance to refer to that object regardless of what's in his mind. And they won't succeed in that.

G. F.:

But maybe someone could tell a similar story about how classic analytic philosophers created all these pseudo-problems, and they got so involved in this language game that they ended up affirming absurdities.

John Searle:

That's right.

G. F.:

Now, if it turned out that you were wrong in considering that meanings are in the brain, would the *Chinese room* argument still work?

John Searle:

Yes. The two are logically independent. The *Chinese room* argument just says that the syntax of

117

the computer program isn't sufficient, by itself, to guarantee the presence of mental content. It doesn't matter, for instance, whether the program is inside the head or outside the head. You'd be surprised to see how hard it is for professionals to get that argument. The reason is that's all they've got is syntax. I tell you, I think mathematicians, more than anybody, have trouble appreciating *The Chinese Room*, because many mathematicians think that's all we do. We just do the syntax; we just manipulate the symbols.

The Background

G. F.:

Would your notion of the background be an alternative to externalism, in the sense of creating conditions of possibility for reference?

John Searle:

I think that the hypothesis of the background, in one way, is in the spirit of externalism, because it says a certain traditional conception that we have of mental content is not, by itself, sufficient to fix reference. They say you need external causal relations. I say you need a set of capacities because the intentional content is not self-

118

interpreting. So there is a level at which the two are in sympathy with each other, but at a much deeper level I think they are profoundly inconsistent. The thesis of the background says that, when the brain works to enable our intentional content to relate us to the real world, more is necessary than just the explicit content. You have to have a set of capacities that enable you to interpret that content, and they're all in the brain. The background is all in the brain. Of course, we're talking about how the brain works at a different level from that of traditional neurobiology.

background
set of
capacities

G. F.:

Are you familiar with the work of John McDowell?

John Searle:

John
McDowell

He's a friend of mine. I tried to read his book. It's very hard. So I can't really say that I know it. He's very intelligent, but his books are very obscurely written. He discussed my work in that Blackwell's volume, *John Searle and his critics*. And I have forgotten the details of what he said, but I remember it was very good. That is, he has very powerful arguments.

119

G. F.:

There are many ideas that are similar to your notion of the *background*. It would be very hard to see where are the similarities and where are the differences. Just to name some of the authors that have similar theories, I will mention Hume (I am thinking of his conception of *experience* and *habit*), Wittgenstein (his idea of *forms of life*), and McDowell, who takes up the Aristotelian notion of *second nature* and claims that second nature is the realm of meaning.

John Searle:

Well, I certainly have been influenced by Wittgenstein. I mean, there's no question in my own mind that my conception of the background was heavily influenced by reading Wittgenstein. Now my colleague, Hubert L. Dreyfus, tells me there are similarities between my views and some existential phenomenologists like Heidegger. I doubt it, but who knows. I think that what they call the background is more like what they think of as *practices*. But for me, the background is a set of *abilities* that generate the practices.

That might not seem to be a big difference, but I think it's a very big difference in the actual analysis because the actual events don't explain anything, but the abilities that generate the events, and the way that they generate the events, have explanatory power. So I'm very reluctant to talk about the background of practices. That's what some of the phenomenonologists talk about. But I want to talk about the background of abilities, capacities, tendencies, and dispositions.

I think there is a similar picture in Wittgenstein. And you're right to see that Hume is probably the first philosopher to recognize the existence of these non-intentional phenomena, which form the causal basis on which we apply intentionality. And I don't think that there's any doubt that that's in Hume's writings.

G. F.:

That's an aspect that is often neglected, as if when Hume talked about experience he only referred to sense data.

John Searle:

Well, he does talk about sense data. But I think he also has the idea that there are these background mechanisms. And in a way Nietzsche is

also about the background. He clearly saw, I think
with a lot of anxiety, that the background doesn't
have to be the way it is. There is nothing inevitable
about it. If could be different. It could all change. It
could all collapse.

So I divide the background of abilities that
enable us to cope with intentionality and enable us
to apply intentionality, into those parts that are
biologically given, like the fact that we eat through
our mouths and we walk upright and we live at the
surface of the earth, and those parts that are
culturally relative, that vary from one culture to
another. Like what counts as inviting someone to a
dinner party, or giving them a gift, or how far apart
from me you stand when you talk to me. Those may
vary from one culture to another.

G. F.:

I believe that, when talking about conceptions of
the background, you also mention Pierre Bourdieu

John Searle:

Bourdieu's concept of *habitus* is like my notion
of the *background*, although he comes from another
tradition. I don't find him very easy to read. He
doesn't always write very clearly.

122

Philosophy of Language

> "We are capable of communicating with each other. This is amazing, if you think about it. I mean, my mouth is just a hole in my face; it flaps open and this racket comes out. But I mean something by it, and you understand it. How is this possible?"
>
> Extracted from "A conversation with John Searle", *Carlifornia Monthly,* February 1995

Language and philosophy

G. F.:

Do you think that the role of language has been underestimated in traditional philosophy?

John Searle:

Well, I think that what has happened, and it really began with Frege in the 19th century, is that we became acutely self-conscious about language, and we began to see that a lot of philosophical problems depended on certain features of language. Indeed, we began to see that the

123

traditional philosophical problems rested on a misunderstanding of the actual functioning of language. And that was a revolution in philosophy, when people became aware of that.

Now, you can go back in time and cite philosophers who said similar things. I mean, Lichtenberg, the German philosopher, thought that there was a kind of metaphysic embodied in our language and he saw the importance of language. So it isn't something that came out of the blue.

But there was a transformation that occurred at the end of the 19th century with Frege, Russell and Wittgenstein. People had previously thought that the way language related to reality was unproblematic. There just wasn't a problem about it. That you have words and these words are associated with ideas, and the ideas somehow refer directly to objects by way of resemblance. That view survived for centuries and centuries. It's, for example, in Locke, Berkeley and Hume. The way language relates to reality was not a serious problem. They took it for granted.

Frege saw that it was a serious problem; and then, once that problem had been raised, it opened up the possibility of both the philosophy of language, where you have general philosophical theories of how language functions, and something that I distinguish from the philosophy of language, namely, linguistic philosophy. Linguistic philosophy was an attempt to examine features of language as a way of analyzing philosophical problems. So both of these really were creations of the 20th century though, as I said, they began, they had their germ in the late 19th century.

G. F.:

That linguistic turn was very much in the tradition of modern philosophy: the subject examining itself, examining the conditions of its own knowledge.

John Searle:

I think that's right.

Reference

G. F.:

Going back to the debate between internalism and externalism. Is this not a spurious debate? I mean, maybe internalists are right about the fact that meanings are in the head, but Putnam is also right in that precise determination of reference depends on a broader process of causation, and

Gustavo Faigenbaum

Burge is right in that community plays a role in fixing meanings.

John Searle:

I think you're right about that. I have not published anything in which I say that, though I do have a chapter in *Intentionality* where I answer Putnam. I think, in fact, that there are two different questions that have run together. One question is, "How does language relate to reality?" And another question is, "When we assess a proposition for truth or falsity, what elements of the proposition do we assess?" Frege assumed that those must be the same question because he assumed that *Sinn*, or sense, both determines reference and forms propositional content. Now recent debates have made clear that those actually come apart. The propositional content and the mode of presentation are not always the same. And you especially see this in modal contexts - contexts involving necessity and possibility. Kripke and others were right when they said that the sense needn't figure in the propositional content when you're assessing it for necessity and for contingency.

A spectacular case of that is given by David Kaplan when he talks about *indexicals*. Take the sentence "I am here now." Any utterance of that sentence will always be true, and it looks like somehow it's analytic that I am here now. But, of course, the fact that this person is at this place at this time, that's a contingent fact. So you get a parting of the way between the necessity of the sentence, or the proposition "I am here now," internally construed just in terms of the meanings of the words, and their use on an occasion. If you think of the proposition as what reports the fact, then it is a contingent proposition that I am here now, even though the sentence "I am here now" can necessarily only be uttered to say something true.

It seems to me that you get a complete split. I was never much interested in necessity and possibility, but I was always interested in the question, "How does language hook onto the world?" And it seems to me the internalist gives the right answer to that. You have to have something in your head, some condition that the object satisfies. Now the externalists point out, correctly, that the condition may not be a set of general terms. It may be, for example, a causal chain, or it may be a causal chain stretching back to an actual thing in the world, or it may be a causal chain stretching back to a baptism. But, and this is the crucial point, the causal chain can only function to fix reference if it's represented in your head. If I think "by this word, 'Socrates,' I mean the guy other people call 'Socrates,'" then my reference is parasitic on other people's and the result may be a causal chain that goes back to the original baptism.

Within the question "How do words hook onto the world?" leaving aside the question of the nature of the proposition, again you need to make a distinction between two different questions. One question is, "Does the means of fixing reference consist entirely in general terms or general descriptions?" "Man is a rational animal" or "horses are equine quadrupeds." Or does it rely on indexical and causal elements? Now that question has to be distinguished from the question, "Is it internal or external?"

And the answer "it relies on indexical and causal elements" does not imply "therefore it's external." The externalists assume it does and that's wrong. It's entirely represented in the head. Now this last part I did say in *Intentionality*, but the other point, it's such an *obvious* point. Frege taught us that sense and propositional content are the same and it turns out they're not the same. They're the same when you have these nice, elegant examples like "the evening star shines in the evening." Then it's all right. But when it comes to cases where you're talking about necessity and contingency, then they come apart.

It's very important and I've never said that in print. Propositional content and sense are not the same. Frege's great message was wrong.

For me, I don't much care about necessity. I think it's a very limited subject. This is another issue and it's a much harder issue. I think Kripke is wrong to think there is a special category of metaphysical necessity. I don't know what that could mean. I think, in fact, there are essentially two kinds of necessity. There is logical necessity, which is linguistic. It has to do with how we use language. And there is causal necessity – what has to happen. Now there are other uses of the word, you know. There's sartorial necessity - you can't wear a polka dot shirt with blue pants, or whatever. And there's etiquette necessity - you can't eat with your fingers. But leaving aside those trivial examples, the basic philosophically interesting kinds of necessity are either causal or logical. I don't think there is a separate category of metaphysical necessity. But to show that would be a big job. I mean, you'd have to write a whole book to show that and I don't want to do it.

Gustavo Faigenbaum

Proper names

G. F.:

Is the turn towards externalism associated with a
certain theory of proper names?

John Searle:

Of course. The theory of proper names that
came out of the Fregean tradition says that the
reference of a proper name is set by the intentional
content in the mind of the agent. And the rival view,
made famous mostly by Kripke and others,
Donnellen for example, is that the meaning of a
proper name is entirely fixed by the causal chain.
And it's the causal chain that determines what the
name refers to. The causal chain is not represented
in the mind of the agent. It has nothing to do with
what's in the mind of the agent.

I reject that. That would have the consequence,
for example, that it might turn out that when I say
"Aristotle," I'm really referring to a barstool in a bar
in Hoboken in 1957, because that's w/here the
causal chain went. And that couldn't turn out that
way. That's a logical absurdity. That's not what I
mean by "Aristotle." It might turn out that Aristotle

never existed, but it couldn't turn out that Aristotle was something totally unknown to me, because it's part of what I think of as my concept of Aristotle that it is a man, and a philosopher, a person who lived in ancient Greece. As I said, it might turn out that it didn't have a reference. But the problem with the causal chain theory is that it allows the mind to set no constraints whatever on how the causal chain terminates. And we do have such constraints.

Furthermore, if you look at how the causal chain actually works, these are the cases that I described in my original writings on proper names as cases where you have a kind of parasitism. That is to say, my use of the name is parasitic on other peoples. So, by "Aristotle", I mean the person you refer to as "Aristotle," and by "Aristotle" you mean the person referred to by the person you got it from, and so on, back to the original baptizer. But that is just one special case of the use of proper names. I think that, in fact, what's true in the causal chain theory is a special case of the description theory, namely that my use of a name will be dependent on other people's views. I don't see that the causal chain theory, in so far as it is correct, is inconsistent with the description theory. But in so far as it's inconsistent, it seems to me not correct. That is, it says that the causal chain need not in any way be represented in the mind of the agent. It's just how it turns out. And that's wrong.

131

Part of this argument already was in a paper I wrote as an undergraduate. I had just finished my B.A. when I wrote that paper and my tutor, Peter Strawson, said, "Well, send it off for publication." And it took three years to get published. But that's when I wrote it, in 1955.

Wittgenstein and meaning

G. F.:

Would you say that there is a theory of meaning in Wittgenstein's *Philosophical Investigations*?

John Searle:

Wittgenstein rejects the idea that we should get a general account of meaning and what he thinks instead is we should think of words as tools, or as instruments used in a game, like a tennis racquet or something like that. They have a variety of uses and the aim of the philosopher is to describe those uses correctly, and when you've described those uses correctly, then the philosophical problems that surround these words will dissolve. You will see that the problem only arose because you were taking the word "know" or the word "cause" away from the language game where it has its home, and trying to

132

find some essential feature that all causes have in common, or some essence of the notion of causation, and Wittgenstein thinks that's wrong.

So far, that seems unexceptional, but there is the following qualification that I'd like to make to that: almost all language games involve representation. That's what makes them language. Maybe there are a few like "hello" and "goodbye" where you don't have a propositional content. But once you have a propositional content, then you have the question of how language relates to reality. And the reason why that has to be the case, is that language is an expression of the more biologically fundamental capacity that the human mind has to relate the organism, to relate humans, to the real world. It's not surprising that language is essentially representational. You'll always get a propositional content, except for very few language games like "hello" and "goodbye" and "ouch" and "damn".

G. F.:

Would then the language game of reference work in the same way across the board?

Gustavo Faigenbaum

John Searle:

Absolutely. If you referred to Socrates in any language game, you still are referring to Socrates. That's crucial. Then you have to ask yourself, "How does it work representationally? What's the form of the representation?"

Here, my views are like Frege's but without the metaphysical apparatus that goes with his theory. I see the meaning of the word as essentially derivative from the meaning of the sentence. It is the meaning of the sentence that is primary because that has a whole set of conditions of satisfaction, and the meaning of the word is just the contribution it makes to the meaning of the sentence. Now, the meaning of the sentence is its use in the speech act. That is, what you can use it to perform. So on my account, speaker meaning is prior to sentence meaning because the function of sentence meaning is to enable speakers to talk. That's what sentences are for. They are for people to talk with.

So, the crucial question is "what is speaker meaning?" It seems to me that speaker meaning is a matter of the intentional content. And the intentional content is defined in terms of the conditions of satisfaction. So I go back to the

134

traditional view, in that I see language as an expression of more fundamental properties of the mind, and the fundamental property in question is the capacity of the mind to represent states of affairs. But it's the representation of the whole state of affairs that is basic, and then the question arises, "Well how do you do that in a publicly accessible fashion? How do you do that in language?" And my answer to that is, you do it by imposing conditions of satisfaction on conditions of satisfaction. So if I want to tell you that it's raining, I make the sounds "it's raining" and the production of those sounds is a condition of satisfaction of my intention to produce those sounds. But now, I don't just produce the sounds. I produce them with the intention that they themselves should have truth conditions. And that, for me, is the essence of meaning. It's the imposition of conditions of satisfaction on conditions of satisfaction. Am I being clear? We are covering an awful lot of philosophy in a very short space.

Social normativity and Wittgenstein's private language argument

G. F.:

This second level of conditions of satisfaction couldn't exist without a social reality.

135

John Searle:

Well, it couldn't exist except for very simple kinds of cases. You see, you have to be very careful about what question you're answering. Now I said that language is an expression of more biologically fundamental capacities in the mind. But, of course, once you get going, you have a kind of bootstrapping effect. And if you've got a language, you can have thoughts that you couldn't have without a language. So my dog can think he's hungry, but he can't think he'd like to go to the zoo next week, or that he hopes I make more money next year, or that I don't have to pay so much in income tax, because those thoughts require language. And a very large number of thoughts can't exist without a language.

So intentionality is more basic than language. But once you've got language, you can have forms of intentionality that you couldn't have without language. The question is, well, when you are imposing conditions of satisfaction on conditions of satisfaction, most of that requires that you share a common language with other people, so that you can communicate with them. Such a set of concepts will enable you to articulate your intentional content. You wouldn't have that without being a member of a society.

But I don't want to say that, without society, you couldn't ever have a very simple kind of language where you just let words stand for certain things. For me, there's no private language argument of Wittgensteinean kind in this. It's just as a matter of fact that the languages we actually speak are social products. They're social constructions and they couldn't exist without a society. But the phenomenon whereby an agent can impose conditions of satisfaction on conditions of satisfaction in the most primitive way, that doesn't require society. That's something that in principle, at least, Robinson Crusoe could do on his island.

G. F.:

Yet, the very idea that there is a normative regulation of utterances seems to me to imply that even the most rudimentary language game presupposes a social order.

John Searle:

Well, certainly, it wouldn't work without a social order. But the actual crucial step in Wittgenstein's argument seems to me not correct. The crucial step is this: unless language were public, there would be no difference between what it seems to me that is right, and what is actually right. There would be no way of telling the difference between "it seems right" and "it really is right." And Wittgenstein says: then you can't talk about right and wrong, and you lose the normativity. I don't think that argument works and here's why: It's true that if I use a word, then I need other people to make sure that I use it correctly, that I use it in a way that is shared by all of us. But it doesn't follow from that, that there's no difference at all between my using the word correctly and my using it incorrectly in cases where there is no outside social check on my usage.

That is, let's take Wittgenstein's case - I'm on an island and I get a certain pain. And I decide to call that pain "s". Now, let us suppose that, unknown to me, it is an angina pain, it's a pain caused by a heart condition. There's a peculiar feel to that. Now I make a resolve that from now on whenever I get that pain I'm going to write "s" in my journal for this sensation, because I want to be able to tell the doctors, if they ever rescue me, what kind of pain I had. Now there are different ways of interpreting Wittgenstein. But in one interpretation, on Kripke's interpretation, this would be impossible. I couldn't do that because anything I write down will be okay. But it's not true that anything is okay. On the contrary, given my background and given my intention, I intended that the expression "s" refers precisely to this quality, this type of pain.

138

G. F.:

But at a point in your argument you say "given my background." There you are admitting that your explanation of what the man on the island does, only works if he already has a certain background. For instance, he has the habit of playing the language game of keeping a journal, using certain marks to denote or represent certain kind of pains, etc., and that's not the kind of activity you would do without a *social* background.

John Searle:

Well, I think that's right, but is that a logical truth or is it just a fact about human development? I mean, suppose you could have put a machine on my head that would have programmed my brain with exactly my present brain capacities. It seems to me that such a machine would have given me the same abilities I have now, but without my having to go through normal development. Now, of course, real human beings can only acquire these capacities by living in a society. But that seems to me a contingent fact about development, about ontogenesis. It does not seem to me a necessary truth about the nature of human capacity. I couldn't get these capacities except in society. But you could imagine that these capacities are realized in

139

my brain and somebody might put a machine on my head that put these capacities in. There's no logical reason why you couldn't put a machine on my head that would give me a complete knowledge of Greek. If you did that, I then would be able to speak Greek. It's just not the way we normally learn languages. In real life you have to practice the language, and be with people, and so on.

Let me just say one other thing about this. You see, the problem with Wittgenstein's argument is that, with any use of a word, public or private, at some point I just have to recognize what is going on. I somehow have to recognize that, yes, this is the same sensation. And if you say, "Well, you can't recognize that without human agreement." Well, *then* I have to recognize human agreement. And the same problem arises. Is your behavior of agreeing with me really human agreement? Or maybe it's like 7 plus 5 equals 125.

It seems to me that Wittgenstein says, "Well, you have to rely on agreement, otherwise anything goes." But, of course, anything goes with agreement, too.

G. F.:

Is it institutional facts that explain speech acts, or speech acts that explain institutional facts? In other words, your analysis of speech acts proves useful for understanding our social ontology, but one could say speech acts have precisely the features your analysis reveals because we are social actors, persons with rights and responsibilities. In other words, it would then be our social world that constitutes the basic features of speech acts rather than the other way around. In that case, we would have a top-down explanation, rather than a bottom-up explanation.

John Searle:

Well, I think this is a very complicated question and I don't think there's any simple answer to it. You have to distinguish different questions. One question is: would it be possible for human beings who didn't have a language to evolve a language just by expressing their intentionality in certain sorts of ways? And the answer to that question has to be: yes because we know language did evolve. There was a time when human beings didn't have a language, and then they got a language, and there must have been a transition period. But now, in our present situation, where we have a full-blown language, what is the relation between linguistic ontology and social ontology generally?

What I argue for in *The Construction of Social Reality* is that language is the basic social

141

institution, because in so far as there are other social institutions such as money, property, marriage and government, they require forms of symbolization which are essentially linguistic. We impose functions on entities where the entities can't perform those functions in virtue of the physical structure, but only in virtue of the collective acceptance or recognition of the entity as having a certain status, and with that status a function. So if you think of money, money doesn't perform its function by virtue of the fact that it's paper, gold or silver. It isn't the physics, but the fact that we grant it a certain status. Now, if that's right, then language must be the essential social institution, because in order that you can impose that function, you have to have some way of representing it. You have to have some symbolic way of representing that this piece of paper has the function of money. It isn't self-identifying as having the function of money. And that move, whereby you impose a function on something can only exist in so far as it's represented, and the representation requires some linguistic or symbolic device.

G. F.:

Some authors (for example Jane Astington in *the Child's Discovery of the Mind*)[3] seem to

---

[3] Jane Wilde Astington (1993), *The Child's Discovery of the Mind.* Cambridge, MA: Harvard University Press. pp. 70-72.

emphasize the expressive content of speech acts, that is, the speech act as expressing the agent's mental state. Thus, to make a promise is to express one's intention to do something. Whereas other authors seem to emphasize the normative aspect, the fact that, when you make a promise, you operate within an institutional reality. The emphasis in the latter case is on the fact that the validity of the speech act can be assessed in terms of constitutive rules and, if successful, the act implies certain consequences in terms of your dealings with other people. For instance, if you have made a promise, you are committed to do something. How do you stand in terms of this opposition between the "expressive" and the "normative" aspects of speech acts?

John Searle:

There's no simple answer to the question. This is related to the question, what's the relationship between the individual and the social? You get a constant interaction and trade off. Every speech act has to be performed by some individual acting intentionally. The only exceptions would be collective speech acts where we pass legislation, or something like that. In the normal case, you and I are having a conversation and each of us has to perform speech acts by their intentional behavior. But the intentions are made possible by the fact that we're members of a society that has a certain kind of institutional structure. So I can't intend to ask you a question, give you an order, or make a promise to you unless I master of a certain type of institutional apparatus that enables me to do that.

Here the analogy with games works. In a game, I have to act individually. I have to act intentionally. I have to kick the football this way as opposed to that way. But, of course, I can only score a goal or even pass the ball within an institutional structure, which is social. Generally, the speech act is the expression of an individual intentionality, but the possibility of my expressing that intentionality is a social possibility. That's the general point.

Some people have tried to analyze speech acts entirely in terms of "expressive" categories such as expressing beliefs, expressing desires and expressing intentions. They think making a statement is just expressing a belief, giving an order is just expressing a desire, and so on. These analyses invariably fail. This apparatus is not rich enough to capture the normative aspects of speech acts. To get to the normative aspects you have to explain the deontology that is built into speech acts and that requires a richer apparatus than just the apparatus of expressing your intentional states.

Austin and Speech Acts

G. F.:

Could you summarize what were your main contributions to Austin's theory of Speech Acts?

John Searle:

Well, that's a question that requires a long answer, but let me go through it. It's important to emphasize that when we read Austin we're reading his lecture notes. He would never have published them in this form, and I know that for a fact, because I asked him and he said "it's too half-baked."

So we don't know what his book on Speech Acts would have looked like. But if you take it the way it is, then it seems to me that the advances that I made were 1) I present a general theory of speech acts and I fit it into the theory of meaning. The nature, extent, and possibilities of speech acts have to derive from the nature of meaning itself. And Austin didn't really have either a general theory of speech acts or a theory of meaning. He had these brilliant insights, but he did not have a general theory. 2) An important feature of the general

145

Gustavo Faigenbaum

theory is that we're to think of the institutions within which we perform speech acts as systems of constitutive rules. There's nothing like that in Austin. And, 3) we're to think therefore that speech acts performed within these institutional structures are institutional facts, that you typically create an institutional fact when you perform a speech act. There is an analogy with games whereby you create a touchdown or you create a home run. Similarly, you create a promise, or you create a command, by operating within these institutional structures.

That seems to me the sort of basic framework that Austin didn't have. Now, within that framework, I believe I did make some improvements on Austin.

First, his taxonomy doesn't work. Basically, it doesn't work because he doesn't have a clear principle for distinguishing one kind of speech acts from another kind. And I think my taxonomy of assertives, directives, permissives, expressives, and declarations, is a vast improvement on his. However, it's important to emphasize that I couldn't have done that without his earlier work. I'm building on the work that he did.

G. F.:

Austin was like an Aristotelian biologist, classifying words as if they were living kinds. Words

146

are living beings, and you do your fieldwork with a dictionary.

John Searle:

That's a good idea. It's a good way of putting it. Austin thought that the way to do a taxonomy of illocutionary acts is to go to the dictionary and make a list of illocutionary verbs, and then see how they cluster together. My approach is to get a theory of what a speech act is and then let the nature of speech acts dictate the taxonomy. It's like the difference between Aristotelian taxonomy and genetic taxonomy. You get a theory of what these things are and then your theory will tell you what are the differences that make something a promise, as opposed to a command, as opposed to a statement. There will be some structural features that determine how particular examples fit into the taxonomy. But you can't do such a taxonomy just by classifying verbs. The verbs may be shaped by contingent facts of English usage. There are lots of languages that don't have many illocutionary verbs. In fact, I have a linguist friend who tells me there's one language in Africa, in which there is only one illocutionary verb in the whole language. It's a verb meaning "to say," but they don't have this range of speech act verbs that we have.

G. F.:

And most likely they perform all kinds of speech acts using other linguistic means.

John Searle:

I think they must have a way of making commitments and asking questions and giving orders, even if they don't have the verbs that name those things.

Now, second, it does not seem to me that Austin's distinction between the illocutionary and the locutionary works. The definition that he gives of the locutionary makes every locutionary act under that description an illocutionary act. That is, you can't distinguish force and meaning because every sentence has some range of forces as part of its literal meaning. That seems to me another failure on Austin's part.

Third, and we're talking now within the theory, there is a persistent confusion in Austin between verbs and acts. When he asks the question, "How many kinds of illocutionary acts are there?" he assumes that any two non-synonymous English verbs, illocutionary verbs, must name different kinds of illocutionary acts. But there's no reason why that

148

should be so. Verbs can be used to name other features. So, for example, the verb "announce" can be used to name all kinds of speech acts, because announcing is making something public in a certain way. It doesn't name a separate type of what I call an illocutionary point. All sorts of different kinds of speech acts can occur in announcements. There is a persistent confusion in Austin between the verb and the act, and it is part of his overall method in philosophy that he assumes that wherever you have two non-synonymous English expressions, they must mark some basic distinction. Well, that may be right, but it doesn't give you a distinction in speech acts, because a lot of the verbs that we use to name speech acts don't name the speech acts by virtue of the type or kind of speech act that it is.

Austin felt that all of the useful distinctions that people make are already encoded in language. But that isn't quite right. There are a lot of distinctions that are encoded in language, but there are other distinctions that we have made, and that we are capable of making, that aren't marked lexically. Austin had a kind of certain teleological view of the English language. He thought that certain types of functions are marked off. If there's a distinction worth making, we will make it. If there are two words in the language, they must mark a distinction. Neither of those is quite true. They're useful beginnings for an investigation, but there are a lot of distinctions that we can make for which there is no lexical mark, and there are some lexical distinctions that don't mark the interesting philosophical distinctions.

Finally, it doesn't seem to me that Austin has a right conception of the relationship between meaning and communication. The perlocutionary act isn't a speech act at all. The illocutionary act is the speech act, and the perlocutionary act is a description of the effect that the illocutionary act has on the hearer. This is shown by the fact that you can have perlocutionary acts that are not in language at all. That is, I can amuse you, persuade you, bore you, annoy you, or exasperate you without saying anything. These are not properly thought of as speech acts.

I think Austin had a kind of genius for getting a basic insight that the essential thing in language is that speaking is engaging in a certain kind of human behavior, in intentionally performing speech acts. That's what I got from Austin. Now, then, the idea was to build a general theory on that. And that is where it seems to me I went beyond Austin. But it's important to keep emphasizing that I couldn't have done any of that without Austin. Austin was the pioneer.

Now I don't know where he got the idea for performatives. Now it may have just been totally original. There are two other sources in which he is, to some extent, anticipated. There's a French linguist named Benveniste, who has some similar ideas. And now we're told there is this German philosopher, who died in the First World War, who had a kind of theory on speech acts similar to Austin. His name is Reinach. Apparently this guy, Reinach, had a theory of social acts that was something like a theory of a speech acts. There is a collection of articles on Reinach, and there is an article on a comparison between Reinach, Searle and Austin. I guess I should read it.

G. F.:

When you distinguish between *conditions of performance* and *conditions of satisfaction*, I understand that the *conditions of performance* are what Austin called *felicity conditions*. Are you not using the term *felicity conditions* anymore?

John Searle:

I was never happy with that term because it fails to distinguish between conditions which are necessary for the performance of the act at all, and conditions were are necessary for the performance of the act in a non-defective style. I can make a

151

statement to you that is defective in that it is insincere, but it's still a statement.

I make the distinction between *conditions on the successful performance* and *conditions on the non-defective performance*. A performance can be defective and still be a successful performance. Now that's kind of ugly terminology, but the idea is that Austin's felicity conditions gloss over that distinction. So I can't make an assertion to you without committing myself to the truth in the proposition. That's the essential condition. But, of course, having done that, I can make all kinds of defective assertions – if I'm lying, or I don't have enough evidence, I'm not in a position to say the things that I'm saying. And those will be infelicitous, but the utterance is still a case of my making an assertion.

Austin's notion of *felicity conditions* disguises the distinction between those that are essential for the performance of the act at all, and those that just have to do with whether or not the act was performed in a non-defective way. And I want to make that distinction explicit.

Now, when I got into the problem of intentionality I found there aren't conditions on having a belief, in the way that there are conditions on performing the act of asserting or promising. So, what I did to

152

analyze *belief*, was just to analyze the conditions of satisfaction in terms of direction of fit, aspectual shape, and so on. Then, you get a distinction in the theory of speech acts between conditions on the performance of the speech act – whether it's an assertion, or a promise, or an order – and conditions on the satisfaction of the speech act. So there will be one set of conditions which are essential in order for you to make a promise, but then there's another set of conditions which are those involved in keeping the promise. Keeping the promise is the condition of satisfaction. Making the promise requires the conditions on the successful and non-defective performance.

Austin's jargon of felicity conditions tended to stick. I think that most people use that jargon. I have never liked that term.

G. F.:

So there are two different distinctions that you cannot make within felicity conditions?

John Searle:

That's right. You need the distinction between conditions of satisfaction and conditions of performance. And within the conditions of performance, you need the distinction between conditions of performance at all, conditions of successful performance, and conditions of non-defective performance.

By the way, there is another thing that wasn't clear in Austin, namely the distinction between the direct and the indirect speech act. That's one of the things that led him to this confused distinction between the locutionary and the illocutionary. Often you perform a literal speech act, the point of which is to make some other speech act. So I say, "It's too cold in here" and I intend that as an order to close the window, or a request for you to close the window. And Austin didn't really see that that's a really different dimension of assessment. I think he thought there's the locutionary act of saying, "It's cold in here" and then there's the illocutionary act of asking you to close the window. But, in fact, that glosses over the crucial distinction. In this case, I can perform the *illocutionary* act of asking you to close the window by performing the *illocutionary* act of *stating* that it's cold in here. And there's no way that he can conveniently say that in his terminology. So that's another weakness.

G. F.:

Now, even though the locutionary and the illocutionary aspect cannot be sharply separated, is it not possible to still distinguish in a proposition the state of affairs stated from the speech act that's being performed? So, even if they're not different *entities*, one could still distinguish the locutionary aspect from the illocutionary aspect?

John Searle:

You could do that. Yes. I mean, a lot of *Austin*'s examples lend themselves to this interpretation. Often you will have a sentence where it isn't clear from the meaning of the sentence which precise illocutionary intention you had. So I say to you, "Leave the room," but that could be either an order, or a request, or an advice. And it's not clear just from the literal meaning of the sentence which I am performing; thus, there is another distinction besides the literal direct, and the non-literal indirect. Besides that distinction, there's a distinction between greater and lesser degrees of precision. You may have intended that not precisely as an order or request, but as advice to a person. I advised you to leave the room when I said leave the room. And you need to be able to mark that distinction.

Austin ran all of these together with the distinction within the locutionary and the illocutionary. It doesn't work. They are different distinctions. One is the distinction between the direct speech act and the indirect speech act: what you say and what you imply. And that distinction shouldn't be confused with the distinction between greater and lesser degrees of precision as they are encoded in the lexical meaning of the sentence.

G. F.:

Was Austin working on a legal analogy when he developed his theory of speech acts? There is some legal jargon in his theory. The very idea of *felicity conditions* seems to me to rely on a legal analogy.

John Searle:

Austin thought that we could learn a lot from studying the law, as he also thought that we could learn a lot from studying psychology. He used both in *A plea for excuses*. He did think that the law was a good place to study language in an action. When we were students, he would say: "It's always a good idea to look at the law because it matters to people." It matters very much what you say. It isn't something where people can be casual or loose. Now he also thought, though, that there's a danger in the law, namely, that the lawyers are forced to reach a decision. The judges have to come up with a decision even when the facts don't warrant a decision. The constraints of the institutional structure require that they reach a conclusion. He thought we had to beware of that, that often judges would say something false just by the fact that they are forced to a decision. But he did think the law was, methodologically speaking, a good place to study.

G. F.:

I can imagine some like Austin fascinated by the idea that the British Common Law accumulates the wisdom of generations.

John Searle:

There is a powerful impulse in England to think that somehow there's the accumulated wisdom of the centuries encoded in the Common Law. I don't know how much that moved Austin, but he was moved by the idea that ordinary language is a repository of a very large number of very important philosophical distinctions and that it's just carelessness and laziness on our part that we don't sit down and sort out those distinctions.

Now it's interesting to try to speculate why the project failed. I mean, Austin's method doesn't go on. There are very few people today practicing philosophy as Austin's advised us to do it.

157

G. F.:

Maybe it's just because it's a lot of work.

John Searle:

That's part of the answer. It takes a lot of work. One of the reasons that people go into philosophy is that they want answers to very large questions. And the impulses that lead people to philosophy aren't the same as the impulses that lead people to do this kind of careful classification that Austin wanted us to do.

There's another reason. Even after you have sorted out all of the careful philosophical distinctions you need to make, which are encoded in ordinary language, you can often still state the traditional philosophical problem in ways that don't involve these uses of ordinary language. You see, Austin thought that if we just paid close attention to the vocabulary, then we would just eliminate philosophical problems like free will and perception. But it often happens that even after you've got the vocabulary right, you still have the question left over. So, for example, he, I think, demolishes Ayer's arguments about sense data. But even if you demolish all of that there is still a question. What's the relation between the actual conscious perceptual experience and the external world? And, of course, Austin would say, "Well, you need to first get clear about why you're saying it's external, and what is that opposed to?" And so on. But even if you got clear of all of that, and you're completely clear about "seem," "appear," and "look," and all of these verbs, there is still the fact that I do have these conscious perceptual experiences and that they are not the same as the material objects I'm perceiving. What's the relation between the two? And that is a serious intellectual question.

Now, interestingly, Austin was willing to listen to that. I said this to him once after a lecture. And we started discussing this in the lecture hall, in the Examination Schools building on a Saturday morning, and we stood there arguing for so long that we got locked in the building. We had a hell of a time getting out of that building because it was Saturday and all the janitors locked up at noon and went home. We finally found a door that wasn't locked to get us out.

But I remember arguing with Austin about just this point. The same point can be made about free will. Austin says: "Well, if you look at the word *freely*, as in *I did the act freely*, that's an excluder, that's a trouser word, and it will exclude various kinds of cases. So you see there wasn't any problem about freedom of the kind philosophers

159

thought." Well, there isn't any problem about that word, but there's still the problem of free will: are the antecedents of my actions causally sufficient to determine that action? And you don't solve that by doing a study of adverbs like "freely," "voluntarily," "of my own free will," and so on. Once you've got all those sorted out, there's still a traditional philosophical problem left. So that's another weakness in Austin. Not always, but sometimes you still have the philosophical problem after you've got the English language right. And he's right to think that most traditional philosophers are very confused about the English language. All the same, that doesn't solve all the problems. Austin's great contribution was not in his detailed investigation of particular words, as everybody else in his lifetime thought. I think his contribution was the general theory.

G. F.:

Anthony Giddens, in the first pages of the *Constitution of Society*, criticizes your distinction between *regulative rules* and *constitutive rules*. He doesn't give much of an argument. But he says that it is misleading to talk about *regulative rules* because *to regulate* means precisely "to control by rules."

John Searle:

I'm not impressed by that argument. Of course, all rules regulate. That, I guess, is a tautology. However, the point I am trying to make is that there are some rules that do more than that. So you need to distinguish between the *merely* regulative and the constitutive. I don't care how you describe it, but you need a distinction between the rule that says, "drive on the right hand side of the road" and the rule that says, "a touchdown in American football counts six points." Those are quite different.

Chomsky and rule following

G. F.:

How does your approach to language differ from Chomsky's?

John Searle:

I'm not sure what Chomsky's views are now, but I'll tell you how it was when I was at MIT, in the old days, when I was first working on this.

First, Chomsky, in those days, believed that there were a set of rules of syntax, and that this was really the heart of the theory of language: you have rules that generate sentences and the most important part of language competence is the capacity to generate sentences. Once you generate the deep structure of the sentence, then you have ways of attaching a meaning, and attaching a phonetic structure to it, so that it's both speakable and understandable. But the basic thing was the syntactic structure. Chomsky argued that we have to be able to specify the syntactic structure of what constitutes a grammatical sentence without any reference to the semantics or the pragmatics, that is, without any reference to what this sentence means, or what it's going to be used for. And I argued that's wrong. You'll never understand these sentences, and you'll never understand the structure of the sentence, if you don't see that it performs a certain function. Now his answer to that was always, "Well, other things could have performed that function too." And that's right. You can hammer with a hammer or with a screwdriver, or all kinds of other things.

G. F.:

Chomsky also made this point by saying that language is an organ and should be studied as such. For instance, if you study the eye scientifically, you don't study how you use eye in everyday contexts, what you do every day, what

162

kinds of things you look at. You study its anatomy, its inner structure.

John Searle:

I argued against that. If you want to understand syntax you must see the syntactical elements as performing functions. Otherwise, many of the rules will just seem arbitrary. So, for example, it's a rule in English that you can perform the passive whenever you have a verb with a direct object. "John loves Mary" gives you "Mary is loved by John." But that's not the case for a certain class of verbs. So, from "Gustavo weighs 80 kilograms," you can't get "80 kilograms is weighed by Gustavo." And that's just regarded as a fact. There are these verbs that don't undergo the passive. Now, I think you won't understand that if you don't see that the reason they don't undergo the passive is because they mean something quite different. Weighing isn't something that Gustavo does in a way that loving is something that John does. And there are lots of examples. That's just one example of this kind of thing where you will not understand the syntactic facts if you don't see how they fit into meaning and speech acts. So that was one difference between Chomsky and me.

Now, a second difference between Chomsky and me is that I thought language was essentially for performing speech acts, for communicating. And Chomsky pointed out, "Well, what about cases where I'm just talking to myself?" Well, of course you can communicate to yourself too. That did not seem to me to be a serious objection.

But a third point, and this was the point we debated over and over for years and maybe it still goes on, is that Noam (Chomsky) postulated a series of rules, which couldn't be rules, because they weren't the kind of thing that could satisfy the conditions on rules. Namely, rules can function causally in the production of people's behavior when they're the kind of entity that you could, at least in principle, become conscious of. People can become conscious of the rules of speech acts, but the rules of universal grammar are not that kind of thing.

G. F.:

Do you still claim that rule following should be in principle accessible to consciousness?

John Searle:

Phrased that way, I think that the answer is "yes." The problem is with the notion of "in principle." A lot of people object to that, Chomsky among them. And what I meant by that is that is has to be the kind of thing that could be conscious. There's a lot of rule following I do unconsciously. I don't think about the rule "drive on the right hand side of the road" when I'm driving in the United States. But all the same, I could bring it to consciousness. Now, at a deeper level, I might have rules that I couldn't bring to consciousness because of brain damage, or depression, or something like that. But they have to be the *kind* of things accessible to consciousness.

The difficulty with some rules postulated in cognitive science is that they're not even the kind of thing that we could be conscious of. They're computational processes statable in zeros and ones. Of course, the hypothesis is not that the child is unconsciously thinking in zeros and ones. That's just a representation of the computational process. And that's not the kind of thing that could be part of the content of thought.

Now, here I'm being Austinian. If you look at our ordinary use of expressions like "He followed the rule," in what cases we would say somebody was following the rule, a lot of features show up that the cognitive science models don't have. One is that the rule-following activity is always voluntary. It's never automatic. You drive on the left or on the right. Secondly, it's always subject to interpretation. Third, there's always a specifiable intentional content to the rule. You cannot describe rule following just in terms of external behavior because the same external behavior might be exhibited by two different rules. And fourth, if it was not conscious, at least it could be. The last feature really incorporates the other features. You have to have the kind of thing that could be conscious, or else it doesn't make any sense to say it involves rules.

At the time of my stay at the M. I. T., my conclusion was that there are no rules of universal grammar. They're just a set of structural features of the brain that make it possible for us to learn some sort of languages and not others. And one of the arguments that I gave for that is that, precisely to the extent that you have an innate structure, you don't need rules. That is, we have an innate structure that gives us the vestibular ocular reflex. So if I shake my head, or move it up and down, my eyes remain focused on you. And you could describe that as if I were following a rule – move the eyeball equal and opposite to the movement of the head. But, in fact, I don't follow that rule. There is a structure in my brain that does this as a reflex. And, similarly, with learning a language, the child doesn't need to follow the rules of universal grammar. He just picks up French or German or whatever language he is learning, and learns the rules of that language. But the capacity to learn those rules needn't itself consist of the mastery of another set of rules. So that was a point of disagreement between Chomsky and me.

Those were the basic disagreements. Now I think, on this last point, Chomsky may be coming around to something like my view. I haven't read Chomsky's latest book, *The Minimalist Program*, but I think he's coming more and more around to this view, because there aren't any rules left. There used to be a whole lot of computational unconscious rules, but now he seems to be backing away from that position. Just looking at *The Minimalist Program*, it appears that he's now saying that there aren't really a whole lot of rules of universal grammar. I mean, he started this some years ago, with the notion of principles and parameters. You had this big piece of machinery and exposure to one language will set it one way, and exposure to another language will set it another way. But then if that's right, there aren't any rules of universal grammar. I think he has come around to something like my view. By the way, he would never say that he is coming around to my view.

What has happened is that, in fact, Chomsky's views are, in some ways, more like mine now than they were then. I argued then that though you need rules to account for particular languages, you don't need rules of universal grammar. Precisely to the extent that the system is innate, that it's built

167

innately into your brain, to that extent you don't need to suppose that the child is following rules. You've got a brain structure. It does the job of the rules. And I think that Noam (Chomsky) has come around to a position that is close to mine.

G. F.:

Would you say that the language – organ analogy is not the right one?

John Searle:

I think there's something right about it, but there's something very misleading and really confused. Chomsky often talks as if a natural scientist might come from Mars and observe human language as a kind of natural phenomenon. But, of course, a natural scientist would never study language, because language is always observer relative. Language is not like gravitational attraction. Something is a sentence of English only relative to the fact that people regard it as a sentence of English. So there can't be a natural science of English, French, or German because those are not natural phenomena. They are socially created phenomena.

However, Chomsky is right in the following respect: there can be a natural science of the capacity that people have to speak a language. But that's a science that studies a certain brain function. And we will understand that science much better when we understand how the brain works. What Chomsky would like to do is this intermediate study of the rules that the brain follows which are not the rules of particular languages, and are not the facts of the neurobiology either. I don't think there can be any such a science, and I don't think there is any such level. And I gather he may be coming around to that view. The natural science analogy is slightly preposterous. No natural scientist would ever study French or German because they're not natural phenomena.

G. F.:

So, the fact that the analogy is not that good doesn't mean that you have to depart from the nativist approach to language acquisition.

John Searle:

I think the innateness hypothesis, or the nativist hypothesis, is true. Chomsky objects to the expression "innateness" but the idea that there is an innate structure in our brain that enables us to learn language, that seems to me obviously right. Just as there's an innate structure in our brain that enables us to see.

I would like to say, and I think I said this already, that I have a good personal relationship with Noam (Chomsky). Yet I think he's, in many respects, profoundly mistaken. And what has happened, it's interesting, and that is that the project never quite came off. See, they've been at it since 1957. That's getting close to half a century and there is no accepted model of English syntax or any other syntax.

Metaphor

G. F.:

Could you state briefly your current view on metaphor?

John Searle:

Well, I take metaphor to be a special case of the general phenomenon where you say something and mean something more, or something different from what you say.

Metaphor differs from indirect speech acts, in that in the indirect speech act, you really do mean literally what you say, but you also mean something more. So when I say, "Can you pass the salt?" I

170

mean "Can you pass the salt?" but I also mean "Please pass the salt." When I say, "You're standing on my foot," I mean you're standing on my foot. But I also mean, "Get off my foot." When I say, "It's hot in here," I mean it's hot in here, but I also mean something more, like "Open the window."

Now, metaphor is different in that the case of metaphor you don't mean what you say. You mean something different, but the literal meaning of what you say is supposed to convey what you really mean, beyond what you say. If I say "It's hot in here," that is an indirect speech act, that could mean "Please open the window." But if I say, "It's hot in here" as a metaphor, describing an argument, then that's a metaphor meaning that the argument is becoming very noisy, violent, too strong, or hostile. The question for metaphor is: how does the intended speaker meaning get conveyed to the hearer when it is not encoded in the literal sentence meaning?

In the article that I wrote about metaphor in *Expression and Meaning*[4], I tried to describe the mechanisms by which a speaker can understand the metaphorical utterance as meaning something more or something different from what the words literally mean. And I gave an analysis that has some

---

[4] Searle, J. R., (1979), "Expression and Meaning," Cambridge University Press, London.

171

relevance for my analysis of indirect speech acts and that involves three stages. First you have to recognize that this is not a literal utterance, that the person who says, "It's hot in here," implies something different from what he says. Secondly, you have to figure out what he might possibly mean. And then third, you have to narrow it down to what he could actually mean.

A lot of people in psychology think that when I describe this logical structure, I am trying to describe actual cognitive processes. And then they do what they always do. They do these reaction time experiments. That's irrelevant. Susan Ervin-Tripp did that with indirect speech acts. The child may learn, "Can you open the window?" before he learns, "Open the window." So the processing time may be the same, or even less, for the indirect speech act. But it's still indirect. And there are utterances that the child will recognize as admitting a literal interpretation. So my hypothesis is not intended as a psychological hypothesis about the time of cognitive processing. It's a logical hypothesis about the logical structure of indirect speech acts.

G. F.:

So you are not committed to saying that every time we hear an indirect or metaphorical utterance we have to go mentally through all the intermediate steps.

John Searle:

No, of course not. No, I am not saying that. I am saying that's the underlying logical structure, but that's not a description of the actual temporal process of cognition. You short-circuit all that. If I say, "It's hot in here," metaphorically, and people are shouting, you get that instantly.

G. F.:

In your article on metaphor, when you talk about the traditional version, you criticize the similarity theory of metaphor. But then, in Aristotle and some other authors, there is a more specific formulation of this theory, namely that metaphor often takes the form of a proportion or *ratio.*

John Searle:

Right: A is to B as C is to D. Yeah.

G. F.:

Would your criticism of the similarity theory of metaphor also apply to this formulation?

173

John Searle:

Yes, I think so. There is a systematic confusion between the strategy for comprehension and the conveyed content. So if I say, "George Washington was the father of his country," the strategy for comprehending that is to see that Washington's relation to his country is like the relation of a father to his children. And that is a strategy for comprehending. But they treat this as if it were the truth-conditions. As if, "George Washington was the father of his country" were a literal statement about the relationships, about the similarity between Washington's relationship with the country and a father's relationship with his children. I think that's the wrong way of understanding that. The proportion does not give you a different set of truth-conditions, it gives you the strategies of comprehension.

The argument for this is very simple. "Washington was the father of his country," isn't literally about children and parenthood. It's about Washington and his relation to the United States. And you see this in the simple metaphors. If I say, "Sam is a gorilla," that is not literally about gorillas. I'm not talking about gorillas. I'm not saying, "Take any gorilla and you'll see a similarity to Sam."

174

That's not it at all. It's a strategy for conveying a new propositional content.

G. F.:

Right. But that flaw of the theory only shows up when you are in the context of analytic philosophy. In Aristotle, of course, there's no talk about truth-conditions. His example is very similar to yours. He's talking about Pericles' funeral speech, which he takes from Herodotus. Pericles says that, in the Peloponnesian War, Athens lost its Spring. Aristotle analyzes this metaphor as based on a proportion or analogy: the Spring is to the year as the youth to Athens. In an analogy the four terms are explicit, but in the metaphor one of them was erased. Since this four-term structure is not explicit, it is the hearer's task to retrieve the missing fourth term. Aristotle says that metaphors are like puzzles, and that part of the pleasure of hearing, a metaphor lies in solving the puzzle.

John Searle:

It might be that the actual historical Aristotle is not subject to the objections that I make. I was confronted with the literature and in the literature it is common to say that there are two general approaches to metaphor – the similarity theory and the verbal interaction theory. And the similarity

175

theory is credited to Aristotle. And then I pointed out that neither of these will quite work. And, in particular, they won't work because they don't seem to adequately distinguish between speaker meaning and sentence meaning. And they don't distinguish between strategies of comprehension and conveyed semantic content. And you're saying that Aristotle didn't think of this in terms of conveyed semantic content, but just maybe as strategies of comprehension.

G. F.:

I think he says simply that the meaning is transferred from the source to the target. He is explaining the meaning of words, but he's not thinking in terms of truth conditions.

John Searle:

That may be right. I don't know enough about Aristotle to have an intelligent conversation.

G. F.:

Why do people choose to speak metaphorically?

John Searle:

Well, there is another weakness in my article and I wish now, if I were to re-write it, I would put this in. There are lots of different kinds of metaphors. I wanted a unified theory. But there are a number of completely different types of metaphors. And people shouldn't confuse the aims of a very elaborate poetic metaphor, or a very subtle poetic metaphor, with metaphors in ordinary conversation. Metaphors like, "Oh that guy's a pig" or "She's a block of ice." Those are not poetic. They're just designed to convey a certain type of semantic content. Whereas with poetic metaphors, you're often invited to have a certain experience from a certain point of view. And those are different motives.

G. F.:

Would open-ended metaphors be more appropriate for poetic than for everyday usage?

John Searle:

Yes. I give an example in the article. When Romeo says, "Juliet is the sun," that's open-ended. He doesn't mean that Juliet is 93 million miles away and made of hot gas, but "My day begins with Juliet.

She brings warmth into my life" or "brings light into my life." It is an open-ended thing.

G. F.:

But there is also an iconic aspect, right? In the sense that not every comparison that will provide the same information is equally appropriate.

John Searle:

No, that's right. And that's the 'seeing as' aspect. You see Juliet as if she were the sun.

Let's list some motives by which people would use metaphors. One is, there's just a semantic gap in the language, and you borrow the term to fill the gap. Computer science is full of this and, indeed, science in general is full of this. So when the first cathode-ray tube was invented, it was called a mosaic plate because it was like a mosaic. You had a lot of little cells and you filled them in. It's a metaphor. The tube does not literally have a mosaic inside... Now that's an example where there is a semantic gap. I think we do this a lot in computer science.

Often in a new science or in a new technology we don't have a word for what we want to describe. So we borrow a word and use it metaphorically. We call the Internet "the web." It is not literally a spider's web, but it's like a web. It's a metaphor. And often we didn't know how to describe the brain, so it's always tempting to adopt these metaphors. Like the brain is a computer. And then you'd get a danger that people would take these literally.

That's one motive for metaphor. There is a semantic gap. People need to fill the gap so they use a metaphorical term.

A second motive for metaphor is rhetorical impact. If you say, "Sally is unemotional, she's lacking in emotional strength," well, that's not completely literal, since there is a metaphorical use of "strength" there. But it's more metaphorical and more powerful if you say, "Ah, that damn Sally, she's a block of ice." It has more force to it.

Language works essentially by a process of recognition of similarities, and that's precisely how metaphors work. So the extension of similarities into metaphorical similarities has no sharp dividing line. A moment ago I used the word "strength." Is that a metaphor or not? Well, I don't know how to answer that. I don't think you can make a sharp dividing line between the way that you're seeing things as metaphorically similar to strong things, and the way that you're seeing things as literally

179

similar to other things when you use regular predicates.

G. F.:

In his treatise on *Rhetoric*, Aristotle says that every time there is substitution of a term for another term, there is a metaphorical effect. If you take that seriously, then it's very hard to tell whether you are before a literal expression or a metaphoric one, because you can say, "I beg you" instead of "I ask you". And that is a kind of metaphor, since it can be argued that one term substituted the other. And if you follow this line of reasoning, then you might conclude that there are no literal expressions, since every term is substituting other possible terms or words that could be in its place. What would you say about that?

John Searle:

Well, I think that's a *reductio ad absurdum* of the theory. You see, you often hear students say things like "All language is metaphorical." But if that's true, it has to be a metaphor because, of course, we understand notions like metaphor by contrasting them with things that are not metaphors - literal utterances. If I say, "This is a table," that's not a metaphor. It's literally a table. When I say, "This is a hat," it's not a metaphor. It's literally a hat. But if I say, "This table is a hat on the head of the rug underneath it," then it's a metaphor because it's not literally a hat and there's not literally a head underneath. So you don't want to destroy the distinctions on which the language rests. The language of metaphor contrasts with literal language, and we only understand those distinctions because we see the contrast. However, there is something right about the metaphorical claim that all language is metaphor - mainly, that language functions on the recognition of similarities. And much metaphor does rest on the recognition of similarities. Not all, but an awful lot of it does. So there is a kind of metaphorical claim that semantic processes are metaphorical, meaning they are like metaphors in certain important respects. If you can't see similarities, you can't speak a language. You must be able to see similarities, and a lot of metaphors rely on the similarities.

G. F.:

Wouldn't some people say that your theory of metaphor is *psychologistic*? I mean, many discourse analysts think that the meaning of a metaphor has to live in the text, and that you shouldn't make any reference to the operations of the human mind in order to explain how metaphors work.

John Searle:

Nothing lives in the text. Speech acts don't live in the text. You have to have an intentional agent. I mean, this is all text magic, to think that the text can do it all by itself. I know a lot of literary critics thought that, but it's a silly view. Anybody who has thought about language has to recognize this as a human form of activity, and human beings have to be able to produce these sentences, these verbal objects, and they have to be able to interpret them. And all of that is psychological. I'm always amazed when people say, "Well, no, it's all just in the text. The author's intention doesn't matter." You couldn't begin to treat it as a text without the author's intention. It's the author's intention that makes it a text.

G. F.:

I think that partly those literary critics are reacting against the idea that the only way to analyze a text is to recover the original meaning.

John Searle:

Yes, some people even thought that you had to psychoanalyze the author. Right. There was a reaction against that. The aim of literary studies was essentially biographical. What you were doing was the biography of the author. And it was, I guess, a healthful reaction against that to say, "Well, look at what the author wrote and don't ask yourself about his biography." But, of course, you can't take this as his writing without looking at the intentionality of it. That it is a speech act at all, that it's a poem, all those are references to the author's intentions.

G. F.:

What do you think of Davidson's theory of metaphor?

John Searle:

He sees one of the things that I argue for correctly. Namely, you mustn't say, as the classical theorists did, that in metaphor one of the words changes its meaning. There's no change in the literal meaning of any of the words. If there were, it wouldn't be a metaphor anymore. It would have a new meaning. And it doesn't. It's precisely because the words keep their literal meaning that you can

183

use them as metaphors. If they change the literal meaning, it would be a dead metaphor and you would have a new literal meaning. The "leg" of the table is now a dead metaphor. There is no metaphor involved in saying, "this is the leg." That's just another literal meaning of leg. It is no longer is confined to animals, but can apply to bits of furniture.

So it seems to me so far Davidson is right. But then he seems to say there isn't *any* account of how an intended speaker's meaning is conveyed, because there isn't any truth condition to the metaphorical utterance beyond the truth conditions of the actual literal utterance. And that seems to me just wrong. In examples I give, "Sally's a block of ice," we might have a disagreement about that. You might say, "No, no, she's hot as a bonfire." And there we'd actually have an argument over this description.

G. F.:

So there are shared criteria.

John Searle:

There are *facts* conveyed by metaphorical utterances and Donald [Davidson] doesn't see that. He does highlight one thing that I don't emphasize sufficiently, and that is that there is a kind of *seeing as* aspect in metaphor. So if I tell you, "Sam's a pig," that means in part "see him as a pig" or "think of him in light of pigs." And I think that's a good point. And I didn't emphasize that enough in my article. I mentioned it in passing, that you get two ideas for one and so on. But I think that it is an important part of metaphor that I didn't sufficiently emphasize and Donald does emphasize it.

G. F.:

Is he emphasizing the iconic aspect of the metaphor?

John Searle:

I think what he's trying to emphasize is that in metaphor you get a literal word that isn't literally true of the object, but you *see* the object, so to speak, through that word. It's like Wittgenstein's *seeing as,* where you see it now as a duck and now as a rabbit.

Gustavo Faigenbaum

So you see him as a pig when you're told he's a pig. I think you can also convey new propositional content because you can argue, "No, he's not a pig. That's just wrong. You've misunderstood him. He's overworked. That's why his room looks so messy. But, in fact, he's a very tidy person. He's not a pig at all." Now that seems to me the kind of arguments we have, and Davidson doesn't allow for that.

G. F.:

What about Lakoff's theory? What do you think of it?

John Searle:

I only read Lakoff and Johnson's first book, *Metaphors We Live By*.[5] I liked the examples. And I liked the idea that metaphors often come in systems. I think that's useful.

But I didn't find in that book any theory of how metaphor works. It was just a list of examples. They didn't have a theory of how a new propositional content is conveyed. And then at the end of the book, they really sort of went off the rails. I didn't see the published version, but they gave me the typescript and at the end they said things like, "So

---

[5] George Lakoff y Mark Johnson (1983). *Metaphors We Live By*. University of Chicago Press.

186

we've refuted rationalism and empiricism. We've refuted analytic philosophy and Chomsky's linguistics and Searle's theory." It was just extreme and they concluded, "And so we've shown that we need to have a new way of organizing society on the basis of smaller communities." Well, they didn't show any of those things. I don't know if they kept these exaggerations in the published version. I told them to take them out. They do, in general, make very exaggerated claims for their theory of metaphor.

G. F.:

There is this volume of essays on metaphor, published by Andrew Ortony. In the second edition there is an article by Lakoff where he tries to address why there are basic metaphors that are recurrent across different cultures. Like "prices rise" or "go up."

John Searle:

And time, there's always a spacialization of time. It would be interesting to know if, for speakers of languages where the text is read from right to left, time moves metaphorically from right to left, because the text does. For us, it naturally moves from left to right. But it would be nice to know if in

Gustavo Faigenbaum

Arabic and Hebrew speaking countries it moves from right to left.

G. F.:

So, what Lakoff says is that some basic aspects of our everyday experience shape our metaphorical expressions. Different cultures share some fundamental metaphors because they share some very general features of experience. I think this nicely illustrates the role played by the *background*.

John Searle:

That's true. I think the *background* is essential for the operation of metaphor. And you may have these universal features of the background, which will give you metaphors that are common across cultures. The temperature metaphors for emotional states apparently are cross-cultural.

In any case, it would seem to be reasonable to suppose that there might be universal metaphors, metaphors that work across languages.

G. F.:

We have already examined indirect speech acts and metaphor. How does *irony* fit into the picture?

John Searle:

Well, I hadn't thought a lot about irony, so my views are probably fairly superficial. But I've always assumed irony is a special case of how sentence meaning and literal meaning come apart, because in irony you mean the opposite of what you say. Indeed, there's a special intonation for ironic utterances. There are cues that you can give the hearer to tell him that you are speaking ironically. Now, this is psychologically interesting because it means that in addition to negation, we have a notion of opposites. If I say, "Oh, he's very intelligent," meaning ironically he's very stupid, the point is not that I simply negate his intelligence, because that would allow for all sorts of things, but I have the notion of the opposite of intelligence.

If I say, "Oh, she's very pretty," meaning she looks awful, then I can only understand that as ironic if I take it as meaning the opposite. The simplest cases of irony are cases where you say A is B and you mean A is the opposite of B. You are not claiming that A is not B but that A is the opposite of B. Now, of course, there are also degrees of irony and this is why we're going to have to make a difference between irony and sarcasm, I guess. There are all kinds of gradations of irony. And sometimes there's an ambiguity. Did he intend

189

Gustavo Faigenbaum

that ironically or not? But you do have the notion of an opposite that's built into the notion of irony.

Rhetoric and argumentation

G. F.:

Would the theory of metaphor work only for the trope called metaphor, or would it also apply to other tropes like metonym and synecdoche, which are "metaphoric" in the broad sense of implying some kind of metaphoric substitution?

John Searle:

In that article on metaphor, I said at the end that I thought that you could just assimilate metonymy and synecdoche to metaphor. But I think that's probably wrong. I think the processes by which they work, things like the *part-whole* relation, are really different from the *seeing-as* relation that you get with metaphor. So I think it's probably a mistake to assimilate metonymy and synecdoche to metaphor. I guess that we ought to go back and re-read all those classical rhetoricians, because they had well worked out theories of all this stuff. They thought their theories were pretty good.

190

G. F.:

Cicero, Quintillian, and Vico…

Okay, are you familiar with Oswald Ducrot's theory?

John Searle:

Well, a little bit. I heard him give some lectures on argumentation, and they were quite interesting. But I didn't see how to map it onto the theory of speech acts. Does he use the theory of speech acts?

G. F.:

He has a strong criticism of your theory. He charges you of letting the propositional aspect stand on the same foot with the pragmatic or argumentative aspect. And his theory is that language is essentially argumentative.

John Searle:

Yeah. That sounds very French to me.

G. F.:

The idea is that you were not radical enough. Yes, it is very French.

John Searle:

Is he saying that every speech act is a form of argumentation?

G. F.:

As far as I understand him, the answer is yes. He says that the meaning of a predicate basically consists in the rhetorical moves such predicate allows you to make. So, if you say, "It's hot in here," then for our commonsense understanding, that is, in terms of our culturally shared *topoi,* that enables the statement "let's open the window," or "let's go to the beach," or "let's buy an ice cream." The meaning of a predicate consists in the set of moves it allows the speaker to make.

John Searle:

That is wrong. The meaning of the predicate is given by the truth conditions, and these other moves are indirect speech act moves. That's interesting. I didn't know that he was that extreme.

Do you know if there's any other stuff worth reading on rhetoric, or on the theory of argumentation?

G. F.:

I like Chaim Perelman very much; he has this monumental treatise on the New Rhetoric.

John Searle:

I met Perelman 30 years ago. He must be very old by now.

G. F.:

He died in the early 80s. There is Stephen Toulmin. There is a Dutch school that calls itself the *pragma-dialectical* school; a guy called Van Eemeren is their main figure, and they publish a journal called *Argumentation*. I don't like them very much, but they are very influential. And of course, I always find it very useful to go back to Aristotle's *Rhetoric*.

John Searle:

I've never read it. You see, my problem is very simple. I read very slowly. I get very impatient. It would take me a year to read Aristotle's *Rhetoric*.

G. F.:

Well, it's not like reading the Metaphysics; it's much easier.

John Searle:

Okay. I'll read it.

From ontology to political science

External Realism

G. F.:

I think some people have problems with your terminology of "brute facts." I mean, how can you talk, after Kant, about a fact that is not constructed by our conceptual schemes or our language?

John Searle:

Well, the answer to that is I am not an idealist. I think the world exists independently of us. It's true that we have to have a set of concepts for stating the facts. We have to have a language for stating the facts. But the facts that you state are totally independent of the concepts that you use, even though you couldn't state those facts without the concept. For example, in English we would say, "The earth is 93 million miles from the sun." Now, in kilometers I don't know what it would be - 150 million maybe. But the point is that it's the same fact in both cases. The actual distance between the earth and the sun is a fact that exists in a way that's totally mind-independent and concept-independent.

195

Gustavo Faigenbaum

You have to have minds, concepts and language in order to state that fact. But the very same fact, the fact that the earth is this distance from the sun, can be stated in different languages and different systems of measurement.

G. F.:

But the very idea of "distance" depends on our being able to move from one point to the other, on the human activities of moving and measuring. Furthermore, the distance can only be specified on the basis of a set of standardized techniques, which in part are conventional.

John Searle:

I make a strict distinction between the epistemology and the ontology. It may well be the case, for instance, that studies of child development will show that unless the child is capable of movement, it will never be able to get the full mastery of the concepts of space. But that's an epistemic point. That's a point of how we know and how we find out. But the question is, "What is it that we know when we know?" We know a certain objective distance, a certain objective fact about the distance between the earth and the sun. So it might be that in order to find out that fact we have to have a certain kind of conceptual apparatus, and you

196

have to be a sort of being capable of certain sorts of things. But it doesn't follow that the actual fact itself, the actual distance between the earth and the sun, is in any way dependent on us.

G. F.:

You say that advances in scientific disciplines like chemistry, physics, or neurobiology leave no room for epistemological skepticism. But, if someone asks you, "Is there a real world out there?" Would you answer, "Just go and open a chemistry book?"

John Searle:

No. There are two things to be said. First, when I say that knowledge is certain, I am not saying that it's incorrigible, because we often have scientific revolutions. And the mistake in our tradition is to suppose that if we had certainty, then we could never be wrong, we could never be shown wrong in the future. And that's not true. Nothing would preclude the possibility of there being a scientific revolution that might overthrow our existing theoretical structures in the way that Einsteinian relativity showed Newtonian mechanics to be a kind of special case. So when I say we have certainty, that doesn't mean that our knowledge claims are never correctable. They are.

197

But I make a distinction between knowledge claims like, for example, "water is composed of hydrogen and oxygen," and the general presupposition that there exists a real world independently of our representations of it. The latter point is what I call *external realism* – the idea that there is a reality out there, which exists independently of us. I take *external realism* not as a theory, but as the precondition of having theories.

Some of the skeptical arguments about realism are of the form, "Well, our knowledge keeps changing." But what that shows is not anti-realism. That presupposes realism. That is, in order that it can be the case that we had a knowledge claim, and we later found that claim to be false, and we adopted a different claim, we have to presuppose that there is an independent reality against which those claims can be checked. *External realism*, in my view, is not a theory, and it's not something you can argue for "yes" or "no." It is the precondition of having theories, because the theories themselves are all intelligible to us as representations of how things are in that mind-independent reality. It is the precondition of having theories. It's not itself a theory.

The mistake is embedded in our philosophical tradition. People thought that the idea that there is a

198

mind – independent reality must be a theory like any other. Kant said it's a scandal that no one has ever proved existence of the external world, and Moore thought he could prove the existence of the external world just by holding up his two hands. I think they were both wrong. It isn't a theory that you can prove and, in Moore's case, he certainly didn't prove anything by holding up his two hands.

G. F.:

Doesn't it all come down to a matter of where you place the burden of proof? A skeptical would say it's up to the realists to prove there is a world out there, and the realist would say it's up the skeptical to prove there is not a real world out there.

John Searle:

If you think of it in terms of proof, you've already made a mistake. I think there is no way an anti-realist can make ordinary claims intelligible. I mean, when the anti-realist goes to the doctor and the doctor conducts tests, and the tests are designed to show whether or not the anti-realist has cancer, then it's not enough for the anti-realist to say, "Well cancer's just a text like any other text." No, he really wants to know, "Have I got this disease in my body?"

199

G. F.:

Hume used to make exactly the same point about how, when you leave the philosopher's office and go back to the ordinary world of human affairs, and you meet with your friends to play backgammon, all those skeptical doubts seem irrelevant and just fade out.

John Searle:

That's right. You automatically have to assume there's a real world. And I think that external realism is not a theory, but it's a condition of intelligibility. It's a condition on the kind of intelligibility that our claims have.

Intrinsic and observer-relative features of the world

G. F.:

I would like to challenge the distinction between intrinsic features and observer-relative features. You maintain that nature knows nothing of conscience or purposes. Why is it so clear that there is no room for teleology in our view of nature? Some philosophers have not accepted a purely mechanical view of nature. For example, Hegel considers that nature syllogizes, in the sense that reality is not just a mass of brute facts, but is rationally structured. To take some other, very heterogeneous authors, Peirce's category of *thirdness* implies that in nature there are totalities regulated by immanent laws. Gregory Bateson has a book called *Mind and Nature*, and also sees rationality and meaning as embedded in nature. The insight these very different authors share is that we not only discover *facts*, but also discover that facts *relate to each other*, forming certain *patterns*, that patterns of interaction constitute *systems*, and that *values* and *intrinsic ends*, *telos*, might be embedded in those natural systems.

John Searle:

You face a difficulty. Namely, what fact about nature makes it the case that it has teleology? No one has made any notion of teleology intelligible except relative to conscious agency. That is, if I am a conscious being, I can talk about my purposes. And if you're a conscious being, you can talk about your purposes. But if you talk about the purposes, let's say of gravitational attraction, or the purposes of the solar system, it can only be relative to some selection of some conscious agent. Unless you want to say nature is conscious... I guess if you're

Hegel, you do think nature is conscious, you think it's all one big consciousness.

If you're like me – I am a realist, an external realist – then you think there's a real world that exists independently of us and independently of all consciousness, and you can't find any teleology in that real world because teleology only exists relative to consciousness.

G. F.:

You were taking examples from physics. But let's take an example from biology. How the cell manages its energy. Or, for instance, take the principle of homeostasis, the fact that some organisms, namely mammals and birds, can regulate body temperature.

John Searle:

Let's talk about this. The best argument against my view is biology. It is irresistible to anybody doing biology, particularly evolutionary biology, to think that somehow or other life and survival are intrinsic values. They're not just things that happen. They are intrinsic values in nature. But I think they misunderstand evolution.

Of course, in doing evolutionary biology we're interested in how certain species have lived, survived, and reproduced, and certain others have not. It's almost irresistible, when we think of evolutionary biology, to think that somehow or other life and survival are purposely built into nature. That the tree somehow is trying to survive and it's trying to produce other trees like itself, and the DNA is trying to reproduce DNA.

But it isn't. These are just natural facts and this is what we learn from Darwin — the appearance of purpose in nature can be entirely accounted for by absolutely biochemical processes and brute reproductive processes. Of course, there are agents in nature that have purposes — humans and conscious animals. But the tree, the cell, and the DNA molecule, have no purposes because they're not conscious. Now there's a paradox here, in that Darwin's greatest achievement was to eliminate purpose from nature, and to show that there was a natural explanation of the appearance of purpose. And people have now reinterpreted Darwin's results to make it out as if Darwin was somehow showing there's teleology in nature. That's exactly wrong.

G. F.:

You mean ordinary people?

Gustavo Faigenbaum

John Searle:

Yeah. And a lot of biologists talk this way. They talk as if we have found purposes in nature. If you don't know anything about evolutionary biology, it looks like the plant turns its leaves toward the sun because it's trying to do something. It has a purpose. It wants to get more sunlight so it can have life and survival. Now Darwin and the whole tradition of evolutionary biology discovered the following. In fact, in place of the initial level of explanation that the plant is trying to turn toward the sun in order to survive and flourish, what we should say is first, as a mechanical explanation, the plant is turning toward the sun because it secretes a growth hormone, auxin, and second, plants that turn their leaves toward the sun are more likely to survive than plants that do not.

Two levels of explanation replace the teleological explanation. One level says there is a causal mechanism. The secretion of the growth hormone, auxin, causes the plant leaves to turn toward the sun, because the growth hormone is secreted differentially in response to light stimuli. The other level of explanation says that plants that do that are more likely to survive than plants that don't. Survival still functions in the explanation, but not as a goal. It's just something that happens. You see? We took the original teleological level - plants are trying to survive and that's why they do this - and we've replaced it with two different levels of explanation. There's a brute causal level. Plants secrete auxin, and they secrete it differentially, and that causes differential behavior in the leaves. And there's another brute level of how this relates to survival, namely plants that do that will survive and plants that don't do that won't survive. End of story. The appearance of teleology was entirely removed. And now a lot of people would like to tell us, "Well, that shows that there's really a purpose in nature and that the plant is trying to survive." But it doesn't show that. It shows exactly the reverse.

G. F.:

Yet, without asserting that there is a conscious purpose, one might claim that there are values embedded in objective systems. The plant doesn't literally need to have any intention to survive. But the laws that explain how living organisms work are not exclusively mechanical laws, but also system laws, principles that regulate and that explain, for instance, this tendency to equilibrium or to certain body temperature.

If you want to explain consciousness, and you only have two levels - the mechanical level of brute facts, and the spiritual level of intentionality, and nothing in between, it does not look plausible that you will ever be able to go from one level to the other. By way of contrast, you can also see nature as consisting in a hierarchy of levels, with different degrees of complexity, where you can have not only physical or biochemical mechanical interactions, but also a specific biological level where systemic principles regulate life. This would be an intermediate level between brute chemical processes and mental processes. I don't know if that makes sense to you.

John Searle:

Well, here's my view. Of course there are many levels in nature. No question about it. You can describe things at the level of quarks, or at the level of subatomic particles like electrons and protons, or at the level of atoms, molecules, cells, and so on. There are many different levels in nature and, in particular, in biology. You want to be able to talk about a whole species, organs within species, specific organisms. So there are lots of different levels.

You want to be able to account for things like homeostasis, which are crucial in the life and survival of certain kinds of organisms. The mistake is to think that, because nature acts as if it has a purpose, then therefore it does have a purpose. I mean, think of the formation of crystals. It's very beautiful the way the snowflake forms, and it's almost irresistible to think well, water molecules are trying to be so beautiful. They're trying to get this hexagonal shape. But, of course, they're not trying to do anything. These are just brute forces of nature.

The question you always have to ask yourself when you're inclined to think there must be some teleology in nature is: what fact corresponds to the claim? Now if you ask me why I am going to such and such a place, I can tell you the fact that corresponds to my claim that I have a purpose. It's about my psychology. But there's no such fact in the cell. There's no such fact in the pumping of the heart, and no such fact in the formation of the water crystals.

G. F.:

But when have an ontological commitment to the existence of an organism, what are we exactly committed to?

John Searle:

Well, you're giving objective existence to some living entity. Suppose it's a plant, suppose it's a tree. You say this is a living tree. In this case, the fact that corresponded to that claim is that there are a lot of very complex biochemical reactions among big, carbon-based molecules.

G. F.:

But there's also a very complex internal organization.

John Searle:

Well, the organism won't function if it's not organized in the right way. Its organization will follow the DNA code, and the way that the DNA code responds to the environment that it's in. And all these are perfectly natural phenomena. None of this is observer-relative so far. It's all just brute physical facts about life and the organism.

When you talk about value, then you're talking about something that is essentially observer-relative. If it were not, it couldn't function as a value. It's only going to make a difference to us if it can function as a value. But for it to function as a value, it has to be something that ties in with our psyche, something that ties in with our situation. So it isn't a failure of values, that they're always observer relative. They couldn't function as values if they were just parts of the world like stones and trees.

Another way to put this is to say that no brute facts in nature could have the consequence of values. To have a consequence for human action and human motivation, you've got to have something more than just a brute fact, you've got to have something that relates to human consciousness. I think indeed it's essential to having a coherent theory of ethics that you recognize that values are observer relative. Many people think that once you do that, you've got the result that anything goes, nihilism, relativism; that it's all subjective. And, of course, that doesn't follow. That's the confusion between epistemic subjectivity and ontological subjectivity.

G. F.:

So there could not be a third category besides intrinsic-facts and observer-relative facts.

John Searle:

Well, I don't know what a third category would look like. There are those facts that exist regardless of what we think, and then there are those facts whose existence is relative to our situation as users, observers, and intentional agents generally.

G. F.:

Isn't this ontology, insofar as it is based on categories like status-functions, and observer-relative phenomena, typical of the 20th century? Would it be comprehensible for someone of the Middle Ages?

John Searle:

That's interesting. I never thought about that. You're probably right that we are very much a society organized around the idea that everything is there to serve our purposes. Nature is there to serve our purposes and, consequently, we find functions in nature. And this is as true of the people who oppose modern civilization as of the people who are in favor of it. So one bunch of people looks at a stand of redwood trees and thinks "lumber," and another looks at a stand of redwood trees and thinks "national park." But both of them are exploiting nature. It's just that they have a different form of exploitation.

We do tend to see everything in terms of possible usefulness. When I make some claim or some discovery about language or about the mind, the typical reaction I get is, "What's the practical application? What can you do with this?" And this is part of this functional obsession that the 20th century had. I don't know enough about the Middle Ages, but my guess is that that was probably not a common attitude. Nature was perceived to be meaningful and not as an object for human exploitation.

Epistemology and intersubjectivity

G. F.:

Some philosophers, from Peirce to Habermas, postulate that knowledge can claim objectivity only in so far as it can achieve intersubjective validity. Is this view compatible with the correspondence view of truth?

John Searle:

I don't know enough about these guys to have an intelligent opinion about their work. But the point that I would want to insist on is this. The notions of objectivity and subjectivity are sources of massive confusion in our intellectual culture. You need first to distinguish between epistemic subjectivity and objectivity. You need to distinguish that from ontological subjectivity and objectivity. Now, ontological subjectivity has to do with the existence of certain subjective ontological phenomenon such

- epistemic subjectivity + objectivity
- ontological subjectivity + objectivity

as pains, tickles, and itches,. and other conscious states. And they're different from objective ontological phenomena like mountains, molecules, and tectonic plates.

In addition to that, we have this other notion of epistemic subjectivity and objectivity. And the idea is that a claim is epistemically objective if it can be settled in a way that is totally independent of the feelings and attitudes of the observers. So if I say, "Water is made of H_2O molecules," that claim is epistemically objective. It's completely objective because it doesn't depend on whether I like water, whether I think it's good, or how I feel about it. If somebody says, "Water in Argentina tastes better than water in California," that's epistemically subjective. That depends on what you like and what you don't like.

I don't know what is meant by intersubjective, but I think it means that you can get agreement about certain things that depend on feelings and attitudes. So, for example, there isn't any doubt that Shakespeare is a better poet than I am. There isn't any doubt about that. But, of course, that is epistemically subjective because it depends on the attitudes that people have. We get intersubjective agreement on that. But I want to distinguish things where you get an intersubjective agreement from

212

things that are completely objective. It's completely objective that water's made of H_2O.

G. F.:

But what is it that makes the claim that water's made of H_2O objective? The scientific tests and experiments are considered as a sufficient proof of its truth only in so far as they can be replicated, in so far as they can be reproduced by independent researchers, by people with different theoretical and practical interests and different cultural backgrounds. That is the only way to grant objectivity to knowledge claims. If you find out that water has this chemical composition, but you don't have a way to prove it and to share it with a scientific community, then it's not an objective knowledge claim.

John Searle:

Well, that's not how I would carve up the territory. The way I carve up the territory is: epistemic subjectivity is a kind of subjectivity where the truth of the claim depends on the attitudes and feelings of the observers. But it seems to me that's not true in the case of "water is made of H_2O." It doesn't matter how you feel about it. It's just a fact. Now it's true that in order to find out about that fact you have to have a certain kind of constitution. You have to have a certain kind of subjective constitution where you're conscious, you're capable of rationality, and so on. But I don't see that as a threat to complete epistemic objectivity because the claim in question doesn't depend on attitudes.

Morality

G. F.:

Okay. Where do moral laws fit into the world? Are they regulative rules, logical rules, or constitutive rules?

John Searle:

Well, I've never written anything on morality and I've always felt that the stuff I read about moral philosophy was very confused. The essential first step is to get a theory of rationality and rational decision-making. And that's what my next book is about. I don't regard this book as a book in moral philosophy, but I think it is a necessary precondition.

G. F.:

So your next book is going to be on morality.

John Searle:

Well, who knows? But it is a necessary precondition of a coherent moral philosophy to have a coherent theory of rational decision-making. I make a number of claims in this book. I claim that a remarkable feature about human beings is that they can create and act on, and be motivated by desire-independent reasons. When you make a promise or an assertion, or make any kind of commitment, you create reasons for yourself to do something that are independent of your subsequent desires. So when I promise to meet you today, I create a reason for me to meet you even if, at the actual time, I don't feel like it, or I'd rather go and drink a beer, or have a coffee, or go back to bed. I now have a desire-independent reason for acting.

Another classic case is our long-term prudence – where I have a reason now for doing something even though I don't want to do it now, like quitting smoking, because I think it will benefit me in the long run. I think that morality is based on the possibility of desire-independent reasoning. Only if you have a theory of morality, like Hume's, that says you can only really act on your desires, that all you can do is act on desire-dependent reason, then I think that you don't have a coherent moral philosophy.

215

Furthermore, I think it is characteristic of human morality that it involves generalizations. And I see motivation and reasons for actions as desire-independent reasons built into the universality of language. So though I don't have a moral philosophy and I haven't really written directly on moral philosophy, I do think that the essential step in the beginning of a coherent moral philosophy is getting the theory of rationality and that's precisely what I'm working on.

G. F.:

You say that rationality implies having desire-independent reasons. Does that count as a definition of rationality?

John Searle:

No, no. I don't give a definition of rationality, but I maintain that rationality is a structural feature of intentionality. And, in particular, if you have anything as rich as a human language, then the constraints of rationality are already built into it as a structural feature. And the same can be asserted even if you have simple intentionality, like beliefs and desires. This applies even to animals: if they are capable of beliefs and desires, then they are capable of rational and irrational behavior.

216

The key element in rationality is freedom. That is, and Kant saw this, rationality only applies where irrationality is possible. The domain of rationality and irrationality is the domain where people are capable of free action, including free decision-making, free thought for accepting or rejecting the truth of the proposition.

I see theoretical reason as a special case of practical reason. Theoretical reason is about accepting conclusions, and practical reason is about making a decision to do something. But both of these are, in a deep sense, practical. Both of them are exercises of human freedom and, though the concept of freedom is different from the concept of rationality, it seems to me that the domain is the same. The extension of freedom and the extension of rationality are the same.

It is characteristic of human beings that, within this domain, they can do things now that will create reasons for them to act in the future. Those reasons are deliberately created so as to be reasons independent of their future desires. That's what happens, for example, when I make a promise. That's the most famous case. But, I think, just about all speaking and language is like that. All speaking and language involves making commitments of various kinds, and those commitments create desire-independent reasons. So that is what I think

217

is an application of rationality – the existence of desire-independent reasons. But it's not the definition.

I don't offer a definition of rationality, but I do say that the constraints of rationality, such as consistency and coherence, are already built into language and mind. So if you make an assertion, you are already committed to its being true, to your being able to provide evidence for it, to its being intelligible and communicable to the hearer. That's already part of what it is to make an assertion – part of what the speech act of assertion is. That was already in my book *Speech Acts*, but I didn't spell it out. Other people have spelled it out in a similar way. Habermas, for example, took my rules of speech acts and said they were general claims. And what I argue now is that you need to go the next step to see that this universality is built into the very structure of language.

G. F.:

Have you already received any criticisms of the book on rationality?

John Searle:

Yes, lots. I got a long letter from Bernard Williams where he criticizes it. I've just been to a conference at Kirchberg, Austria where the book was the subject of a symposium at the Wittgenstein conference. And I had criticisms by Barry Smith, Joseph Moural and Leo Zaibert. I gave it as a series of lectures at the Jean Nicod lectures in France and there were a lot of criticisms on the spot. And then, of course, it started getting reviews in Spanish because an early version of the book, *Razones para Actuar*,[6] already exists in Spanish. The book is out and is in bookstores in Spain. And people came to my lectures in Paris and they said, "But look. I already have the book. It's all in here." I answered: "That's just the first draft."

G. F.:

So what are they attacking?

John Searle:

Everything. I mean, what makes philosophy fun is that all kinds of things get attacked. People say that my account of desire-independent reasons is wrong. People say that my account of free will is wrong. There are all kinds of attacks. And, of course, whenever you criticize any other philosopher, those other philosophers always say, "You have misunderstood me."

---

[6] Razones para actuar. Madrid: Editorial Nobel: 2000.

Bernard Williams says I misunderstood him. It could be. The debate that I'm having with him is about internal and external reasons. Here I use "internalism" with a different meaning of this word, from the one it has in the philosophy of language. In the philosophy of language I am an internalist. Where rationality is concerned I am an externalist because I believe there are external facts in the world that provide rational grounds for action, even in cases where those external facts are not acknowledged internally by the agent. If you had made a promise, then whether or not you have any desire to keep the promise is irrelevant. You have created a reason for action.

Social ontology, political philosophy and socialism

G. F.:

Is the field of institutional facts homogenous? Let me explain what I mean. When doing research on children's social interactions, we had to distinguish between institutions in a broad sense, like promising, swearing, borrowing, barter, and so on; and institutions in a strict sense like the school, the church, the police. In our account, in order to have an institution in a strict sense it is not enough to have constitutive rules, but you also need an

220

organized body that enforces the rules through power structures and a hierarchy of official positions, such as school principal, teacher, etc. So, would your theory of institutions be compatible with such distinction?

John Searle:

Yeah, it would. What I was trying to do was get at the basic structure that underlies all institutional reality. I make a very strong claim. Namely, that all institutional reality is a matter of the collective imposition of what I call status functions. Functions that are imposed on an object or on a person, a building, or a piece of land, where the object can't perform the function just in virtue of its physical structure, but requires collective recognition that the object has a certain status; and, with that status, a function. I think that is absolutely universal – across all institutional reality, or so I claim.

Within that, then, you're going to have to have much more fine grained distinctions between different kinds of institutional structures, and so you seldom just have a single status function, but you have a whole body of interrelated status functions to serve some other purpose. To serve the purpose of education, you have the function of the teacher and the principal, and the school janitor, and all of these are designed to serve the overall function of the

221

school. That seems to me the right way to look at it. And then you have other institutions that pervade everything, including language or property. I mean, even in the school, it's still my shirt, my shoes. So you have these general institutions that run through society, such as money, property, and language. And then you have specific institutions, such as a ski team, or a school, or a university. And I think this is a rich field of investigation. I've only really got into this in the past few years in a systematic way, and I'd like to develop it further. I think if we followed it out, we'd get a different kind of political philosophy from the one that has been traditional in our society and I'd like to, if I get the time, I'd like to follow it out.

G. F.:

What's your intuition?

John Searle:

My intuition is this. The problem with political philosophy in our tradition is that it does not proceed from a prior political ontology. And the consequence is that political discussion tends to be either very abstract or very concrete. So we ask questions like, "What is justice?" or "What is a just institution?" Or we ask questions like, "Who's going to get elected?" That is, day-to-day journalism. We oscillate between Plato and the daily newspaper. And I think there is room for what I call a political philosophy of the middle distance, where you can discuss institutions in terms of the fundamental ontology of the institution. And I see the ontology as prior to the normative questions about it, like "Is this a just institution or an unjust institution?" You can't really answer that without looking closely at the ontology of the status functions.

I'll give you some examples of this. The leading problem for me in the historiography of the 20th century is, "Why did socialism fail?" Now this to me is personally interesting, because I thought of myself as a socialist when I was an undergraduate. And if I told you the definition of socialism that we had, I think it still sounds very reasonable. But it just didn't work.

Here's the definition: in a socialist society, you have to have social or public control of the means of production. You can't let the means of production fall under the control of a very small number of very rich people. Secondly, you have to have some kind of elimination of the huge differences in wealth. You cannot have a healthy society where you've got one guy who has $20 billion and the other guy can't pay his rent. That's not a healthy society. Third, you have to have an elimination of class differences. People ought to be able to deal with each other on

223

Gustavo Faigenbaum

the basis of equality. And, fourth, everybody ought to have some responsibility to contribute to the general welfare.

Those sound pretty good to me. But the truth is, the effort to carry those out in practice failed everywhere. Attempts to implement this were either just a simple failure or a total catastrophe. Of course, the Communist party failed spectacularly. But Democratic Socialism, which is more interesting because it isn't obviously evil in the way that I think Marxist Socialism was, also failed everywhere. Now, maybe there are isolated pockets I don't know about. Maybe somewhere, there are living models of socialist communities. But in the countries I know, in France and Great Britain, where they tried hard to implement Socialism, it was a failure. Why?

I don't think there's a simple answer to that. To answer that question we'd have to understand better the ontology of economic status functions. If I had several more lifetimes, I'd like to investigate that. I think that's a fascinating set of questions.

Now, you asked me what would political philosophy look like from this point of view. Well, political philosophy is often about power, but it's not recognized among political philosophers that all power comes from below. That's a strict consequence of the logical structure of status functions. If people don't accept it, it doesn't work. This is disguised from us by the fact that power is exercised from above. And since the guy on top is exercising the power, we think somehow or other he must be the source of the power. But there come crucial moments when suddenly it's naked and visible. This happened in the streets of Moscow with Gorbachev, when it was just in the hands of the people, "which way are you going to go"? Or after the attempt on Hitler's life when they called these officers in Berlin and told them, "The Führer 's dead. Now you have to take my orders." And which way would they go? And then Hitler got on the phone and reasserted his authority. And the most spectacular case of all, of course, was in 1989, when suddenly status functions were no longer recognized.

G. F.:

It happened again a month ago in Yugoslavia.

John Searle:

That's right. Exactly. Here's this guy Milosevic, he's been exercising power and it looks like he has absolute power, but the moment that it's no longer recognized, it's finished. It's over. This is a slogan, maybe it's a cliché, but the point I want to make is there's a strict logical analysis according to which all

225

power must come from below. That's not just an accident. It's as true of dictatorships as it is of democracy. And, of course, it's in the nature of power that it has to be exercised from above. So you get this tension within power structures.

I don't understand the notion of leadership. There must be some literature on this that I am just ignorant of. Leadership is a very peculiar kind of status function because it is not just simple power. Power is the ability to make people do something even if they don't want to do it. But leadership is the ability to get people to want to do something they wouldn't otherwise have wanted to do. And often, the most powerful leaders, like Churchill or Hitler, are the leaders who have the ability to get people to do things, which they wouldn't otherwise have wanted to do. So you don't have to make them do them. So anyway, those are just very superficial thoughts that I'd like to discuss in an eventual book about political philosophy.

G. F.:

So, it's interesting how in a completely different domain, once again the microlevel constitutes the higher levels.

226

John Searle:

Absolutely. In a way, all my life I've been writing one book. It just has different chapters. And if you think it through, you'll see that what I'm telling you now is already implicit in *Speech Acts*. It's just that I didn't see it then. I didn't see that in *Speech Acts* there was a theory of intentionality and a theory of social reality. But you keep constantly working out the next consequence. I mean, this is the extension of the microstructure of a speech act on a much larger scale.

Gustavo Faigenbaum

Prospects

American pragmatism

G. F.:

Is there any connection, or are there any shared theoretical positions, between the American school of Pragmatism and ordinary language philosophy?

John Searle:

I don't think so. I don't know enough really about the American pragmatists to have an intelligent opinion. But my impression, from reading Dewey and some William James, is that they thought they had a new way of dealing with a certain class of traditional problems, like the problem of truth. They emphasized function or usefulness or practical considerations. And that's quite different from the Ordinary Language school, which thought that what we should do is examine the ordinary use of words and this will help us to solve philosophical problems. So I don't see a connection there.

You might find probably some minor connections in some minor specific points. But I'm

Gustavo Faigenbaum

very anxious to insist on total objective external realism, and the correspondence theory of the relation of language and reality, and the correspondence theory of truth. And I don't think you get that in pragmatists.

Influence on Child Psychology

G. F.:

Your theory of speech acts has been immensely influential not only in linguistics or in the philosophy of language, but also in the social sciences, in psychology, and in other disciplines. Are you familiar with some of those appropriations?

John Searle:

I probably don't know enough about them, but I'm pleased that the theory of speech acts has proved useful in other disciplines. I know you mentioned earlier Jerry [Jerome] Bruner. He's a friend of mine, and I think he's just splendid. And he makes very good use of these notions. And I have seen references to the theory of speech acts in social psychology, and I'm even told they use it in child speech therapy. That it's useful to have this theory so you can know what constitutes a healthy child where its speech is concerned.

230

G. F.:

In psychology there is a recognition that the theory of speech acts is useful, but I believe that, in the specifics, some authors make important mistakes.

There is, for instance, Bruner's book on *Child's Talk*[7], which presents one of the finest and most influential investigations on language acquisition. Now, Bruner says that an important part of learning a language is learning the speech acts' felicity conditions. He says that if the child asks for a cookie at the wrong moment, for example right after having lunch, then the felicity conditions of requests are violated. Also, Bruner says that the child has to acknowledge that the other person could have the right to refuse to give him a cookie, and that the child has to thank for the cookie if the adult does give it to him. When I was reading this, I thought that the examples Bruner gave were instances of regulative rules, like the rules of politeness. And that they had nothing to do with the felicity conditions of speech acts.

---

[7] J. Bruner (1983). Child's Talk: Learning to Use Language. Oxford: Oxford University Press.

John Searle:

That is what it seems to me like. But I haven't read Bruner on this, so I shouldn't comment. I don't know the work.

G. F.:

Another very influential work is Baron-Cohen's (1989).[8] He says that before acquiring language children engage in some social behaviors that somehow anticipate their future linguistic and social abilities. He specifically identifies two types of behaviors that he calls proto-declaratives and proto-imperatives. A proto-imperative is an act of asking for something, like when the child extends his arm towards an object, makes some sounds or a gesture of effort as if trying to reach it, and looks at the adults nearby so that they give the object to her. A proto-declarative is the act of pointing to something, or somehow indicating or referring to an object. For instance, a kid peering through a window points to a red car, smiles, and looks at her mother, trying to share this focus of attention with her. The kid tries to share her focus of interest with the adult.

---

[8] Baron-Cohen, S, (1989) Perceptual role-taking and protodeclarative pointing in autism. British Journal of Developmental Psychology, 7, 113-127.

John Searle:

Why is that a declarative?

G. F.:

That's exactly my question. A proto-declarative has nothing to do with utterances such as "I declare" or "The session is open." It is more like stating something: "here goes a red car!"

John Searle:

I mean, there is the proto-imperative. I know, because grown-ups told me this is what I did when I was a prelinguistic infant. I didn't speak until very late, until I was two and a half. And my relatives were worried, except my mother. My mother was a doctor and she thought it was completely normal and nothing to worry about. Everybody else was worried. And what I would do instead of speaking was, I would point at something and grunt. "Ugh, ugh." Meaning, "give it to me." And then if they didn't give it to me I would cry. That was a kind of proto-imperative. I was asking for things even though I didn't speak. And then when I started to speak, it came very fast. But I did not actually say any words before the age of two and a half and then I never stopped after that.

233

G. F.:

I bet that's the very origin of your concern with language.

John Searle:

Yeah. Now, I think that prelinguistic infants, or infants who are just developing language, do have this kind of basic imperative. But why would they call the other a declaration? I don't know. It's like an assertive.

G. F.:

The domain-specificity approach is now the dominant view in cognitive developmental psychology. Some authors go as far as to assert the existence of different cognitive modules, each of which operates in a specific cognitive domain. Are such views in contradiction with the philosophical thesis of the unity of consciousness?

John Searle:

No. What the modular theory says is that you have separate mental faculties and, in a trivial sense, that has to be right. My ability to see things is different from my ability to hear things even though they interconnect in various ways. But the thesis of the unity of consciousness says that any conscious state, such as my feeling of pain or my feeling an aftertaste of coffee in my mouth, can only exist as part of a unified conscious field. So you don't have seventeen independent conscious experiences, but rather you have them all together in one big conscious experience and that's the unified field of consciousness. So the thesis of modularity is not inconsistent with the thesis of the unified field of consciousness.

Habermas

G. F.:

Habermas also draws upon your theory.

John Searle:

What Habermas does with the theory of speech acts is, essentially, to take my rules on speech acts concerning the sincerity conditions, the preparatory conditions, and the essential conditions, and declare them to be universal rules of validity. *Geltungs Anspruche* is the German. I think that's interesting. I think that's a useful application of the theory. Whenever we speak we are engaged in following perfectly universal rules. You can't make an assertion in any society without committing yourself in certain ways.

Habermas has a political aim that I don't have. He wants to provide a rational basis for a Marxist critique of society. I am not sympathetic with Marxism, but I think Habermas is right to see that there are general implications of the theory of speech acts. I would want to go one step beyond what he did and say that not only do you have universality built into the rules of speech acts, you also have universality built into the internal structure of the proposition. So, if a man comes to the door and I say, "That's a man," then I am committed to recognizing similar things as men. There's a kind of categorical imperative about the use of any general term. So the situation for me is quite different from the situation for my dog, because my dog can see a man at the door and I can see a man at the door, but once I say there's a man at the door, I am committed to recognizing that other people in a similar situation would be justified in claiming that there is a man at the door.

That has enormous implications for what used to be called moral philosophy because if I say, "Look, I am in pain and, therefore, other people have a reason to help me," then I am committed by the very universality of language. I don't need to appeal to any general moral principles. I am committed by the universality of language to recognizing that in a similar situation I would have reason to help them. So my only objection to Habermas is that he didn't go far enough. I would go even farther.

G. F.:

I wouldn't say that Habermas, nowadays, has a Marxist political agenda. I think he's rather committed to defending the values of the Enlightenment, but without the metaphysical apparatus that was the foundation of XVIIIth and XIXth century Enlightment philosophy.

John Searle:

Well, I may be misunderstanding him. I thought that Habermas was sympathetic with a certain kind of neo-Marxism, but maybe that's not true.

G. F.:

He does come from the Frankfurt school, so certainly he has a Marxist background. But I think that his later writings do not fit into the traditional definition of Marxism.

Gustavo Faigenbaum

John Searle:

It means something in America if you describe yourself as a Marxist. And when I taught in Frankfurt, it seemed to me that neither Habermas nor Apel were Marxists in that sense. To be a Marxist, of the kind that I knew, you have to want to kill a very large number of people. Jürgen Habermas and Karl Otto Apel don't want to kill anybody as far as I can tell. Marx's idea of a violent revolutionary overthrow of bourgeois capitalism seems to me very alien to their style of behavior and their style of life. But I've heard them described as sympathetic to Marxism, and I got the impression that they thought there was something in Marx.

G. F.:

I think that they share with Marxism a critique of modern society as causing alienation, but not the agenda of a violent revolution.

French post-modern thought

G. F.:

The post-modern and post-structuralist thinkers also make use of some of your notions.

238

John Searle:

Well, I had a disagreement with Derrida, and I *Derrida* thought, frankly that he was hopelessly confused about speech acts. I also have encountered *Lyotard* Lyotard. These are not very influential thinkers in contemporary philosophy, but I gather they are much admired in literary studies. But I have some familiarity with their views. I read Lyotard's book on *The Post-Modern Condition*, and I've read a number of things by Derrida. However, I'm certainly no expert on their works.

On the other hand, I knew fairly well Michel *Foucault* Foucault because he was a colleague in Berkeley. And once, Michel was having lunch with my wife and me. And I said to him "Michel, *pourquoi tu écris si mal*?" "Why do you write so badly? In conversation, you're just as clear as I am. There's no reason for you to write so badly. Why do you write so obscurely?" And he said, "If I wrote as clearly as you do, French reviewers would think it was childish. They would say it's *infantil*." He said, "In France you have to have at least 10% incomprehensible." "*Au moins dix pour cent incompréhensible*. Otherwise, they think it's too simple. They think it's too childish. They don't take it seriously. They think it's not deep."

239

I didn't know what to think. I thought, "Maybe Michel is making fun of me or just joking around." So when I was lecturing at the Collège de France, I told this story to Pierre Bourdieu. Pierre was the guy who invited me. I asked him if Michel was serious. And Pierre got very excited and said, "Absolutely right. In fact, it's more than 10%. It's a lot more than 10%. You have to be incomprehensible or people in France won't take you seriously." So that's a difference between France and Anglo-Saxon countries. I try very hard to write everything very clearly.

In France there are a very large number of different sorts of intellectual groups and the ones that are the most famous in the United States are not the best ones by any means. Probably the best is a group of people who do, in effect, analytic philosophy. Until recently, they did it under the auspices of something called CREA, *Centre de Recherche en Epistémologie Appliquée*. And there are a lot of very good philosophers there such as Francois Recanati and Dan Sperber. And there are other good philosophers in Paris as well, like Jacques Bouveresse, for example.

G. F.:

I read what Sperber wrote on the epidemiology of ideas. I don't like it.

240

John Searle:

Yes, I was also disappointed with Sperber's analogy between the spread of ideas and the spread of a disease.

G. F.:

And it's also very simplistic. I mean, you wouldn't like it at all because he compares the individual human being to a computer. And we're all connected to a network. Language is the common communication protocol for transmitting ideas. And *See Dawkins + Dennett* there is a Darwinian struggle for survival among ideas. The survival of the fittest. And that's basically how he's supposed to overcome both empiricism and rationalism.

John Searle:

The point about people like Sperber though, is that he's not an obscurantist. I mean, he tells you what he thinks. It may be mistaken, but at least he he's clear about it.

But then there are other people I admire in *Bourdieu* France. I like Bourdieu, I think he's a very intelligent man. He was my host when I was at the Collège de France, and he's done a lot of good things for

241

me. I did like and admire Foucault. I thought that a lot of what he wrote was loose. He had some confused ideas about realism, about basic philosophical assumptions, but still he had some good insights. The French philosophers that I regard as the most confused are people like Derrida and Lyotard. But they're not dominant figures in France by any means. I gave a series of lectures at the Collège de France in Paris last summer and I found that nobody much talks about post-modernism or deconstruction.

Serious French intellectuals have more interesting things to do. So I don't, for a moment, suppose that all French people are alike; and certainly Ducrot is a guy you can talk to. He is an important linguist and has important things to say.

G. F.:

Have you ever tried to read Lacan?

John Searle:

Yes, I think his writing is just awful. I don't know how anybody can take it seriously. I guess he's no worse than Althusser.

242

Derrida

G. F.:

You had a famous controversy with Derrida.

Derrida

John Searle:

If you read Derrida, you will find a massive fallacy that occurs over and over. It's almost gibberish. But here's how it goes.

Derrida purports to find certain traditional oppositions in Western intellectual life, Western philosophy. Those are such oppositions as those between literal and metaphorical, fact and fiction, men and women. And, of course, he is right that there are a series of dualistic oppositions. And then he says, which is more doubtful, that the one term is always, in his expression, "privileged." One term is always supposed to be better than the other term. Literal is better than metaphorical, men are better than women, etc.

So there's always this privileging of one term rather than another. And sometimes that's true. I mean, obviously we do prefer truth to falsehood. But then he makes a very peculiar move. Here's

Gustavo Faigenbaum

how the move goes. If you have these two terms, A and B, and A is privileged over B, he wants to reverse that and show that B is really the primary term. And the way he reduces it, the way he makes this inversion is as follows. He says, "Given A, B is always possible." Given the literal utterance, metaphor is always possible. Given non-fiction, fiction is always possible. And then he says, "But that possibility is a necessary possibility." It's a necessary possibility that something be fictional given that it's non-fictional. There is always the necessary possibility that it could be fictional. Or, given money, the possibility of counterfeit money is a necessary possibility. And then he says, and this is where it just becomes kind of nonsensical, "Because the possibility is a necessary possibility, somehow or other the B term is already inscribed in the A term." Somehow man is already woman, nonfiction is already fiction, truth is already falsity, and so on with all of these other cases. You justify the inversion by showing that the devalued term is already, in some sense that he never explains, inscribed in the other term.

The problem with this is that it's just silly as a piece of modal logic. In some modal systems, *possibly P* implies *necessarily possibly P*. Mp → LMp. That is in Lewis's S5 and it's probably in S4 as well. But you have to take seriously modal logic if you're going to try to play these games with the

244

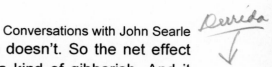

modal operators, and he doesn't. So the net effect is a kind of hot air. It's a kind of gibberish. And it works well, apparently, with literary people. But philosophers remain unimpressed by this.

That's the argument I find over and over in Derrida. This was first pointed out to me by Kevin Mulligan. The aim is to try to show that the devalued term is really the superior term. And the way you do that is you show that the possibility of the devalued term is somehow contained in the privileged term. And then you show that the possibility is a necessary possibility. And then you show that somehow or other the necessity of the possibility proves that (and here it gets very obscure) the devalued term is somehow already contained in the privileged term. Now I make this sound a lot clearer than it is in Derrida, but no matter which way you look at it, it's just a terrible piece of logic.

Another piece of gibberish in Derrida is his argument about what he calls "iterability". Here is how it goes. Any mark (such as a sentence) can be used on different occasions for different purposes. So if I find a note, for example, on which is written the sentence "I have forgotten my umbrella" I could use that sentence for all kinds of purposes. I could use it to practice pronunciation or to call my dog with. So, says Derrida, this proves that the original intentionality of the author of the note has lost

Gustavo Faigenbaum

control of the meaning of the utterance and consequently the whole system of distinctions, between sentence meaning and speaker meaning for example, is undermined or overthrown.

The argument is so bad one does not know where to start criticizing it. Derrida clearly has not grasped the type-token distinction. The fact that I can use different tokens of the same type for different purposes has no such spectacular implications. He is just confused.

G. F.:

I think that Rorty says there is something valuable in what Derrida is saying, but we shouldn't take him literally.

John Searle:

Is that how Rorty wants us to respond? How are we supposed to know what is valuable? See, I have another problem with Rorty. If you look at Rorty's work, it seems there's a massive contradiction on every page.

For example, Rorty says we should strive for democracy and we should value democracy. But then he says, "But I reject the distinction between appearance and reality." But you can't be for

246

democracy unless you're prepared to make the distinction between real democracy, and these phony or fake democracies, like the Peoples' Democracies or the totalitarian democracies of European Fascism and Communism. They typically call themselves democracies, but you'd have to say that's just an appearance. It's not really a democracy.

Rorty says, "Well, you know, I reject the distinction between truth and falsity." And then he says things that, we're supposed to think, are true. You find this glaring contradiction on every page. And I finally figured it out. Rorty has no first order philosophical problems. When he says, "I reject the distinction between appearance and reality," what he means is, he rejects what Plato and Descartes say about it. When he thinks of the distinction between appearance and reality, he doesn't think about real democracies as opposed to fake democracies. He thinks about Plato's cave, and about Descartes on clear distinct ideas. He thinks philosophy is essentially about dealing with such traditional texts.

I am actually interested in the ground-floor problems. For example, I collect oriental rugs and I have to be interested in the distinction in a real Kazak and a fake Kazak. When I think about the distinction between appearance and reality, I think

247

about real rugs and fake rugs. That, for me, is a ground-floor problem. And if somebody says there's no distinction between appearance and reality, he's never been a rug collector. Or he's never been a professor trying to grade students' papers.

G. F.:

Neither Rorty nor Derrida would accept counterfeit money as payment.

John Searle:

Exactly. But they think that there aren't any philosophical problems except these problems that come from the texts of other philosophers. And that's really what's wrong with Rorty. He has no first order philosophical problems. There are almost no direct first order philosophical problems in Rorty. It's all about other philosophers. And I think the same is true of Derrida. The talk is all about this intertextuality. It's not about ground-floor problems.

G. F.:

What's the story behind Derrida's book *Limited Inc.*?

John Searle:

He wrote an article about Austin. And some people came to me and showed me this article, and asked me what I thought of it. And I read it and told them what I thought of it. And they then said, "We're starting a new journal, the purpose of which is to encourage communication between Anglo-Saxon and Continental Philosophy. Would you write up a few notes? Would you write this up and let us publish this?" I didn't see any objection to that, but I didn't realize I was being set up. This was a trap.

The purpose of the journal was to celebrate this sort of deconstructionist nonsense and they wanted me to provide a target for Derrida. They didn't tell me that. So I wrote a nine-page article. I wrote it on a weekend. And I'm told that Derrida spent six months writing this huge reply to my article, in which he spends the first twenty pages misspelling my name and so on. But I can't take it seriously. It's not a real work of philosophy, and I'm amazed that it was published. The journal has since gone out of business.

Derrida's original article appeared in issue number one of this journal called *Glyph* together with my reply to it. Then, six months later or maybe a year later, without telling me, this huge thing by

Derrida was published – over 100 pages in typescript– supposedly in response to me, and I thought it was ridiculous. I didn't think it was worth replying to, so I never replied to it. And then, to my amazement, Derrida wanted to make a book out of this. I don't think it's worth a book. It doesn't have enough intellectual content for a book. But it was published as a book in Paris, and I guess they did a translation in the United States.

G. F.:

Did he want your article to appear in his book?

John Searle:

I wouldn't allow it. I don't want to encourage these people. I wrote another article in which I attacked him. And that was an article where I actually said what I think about deconstruction. That was called *The Word Turned Upside Down*. It appeared in the New York Review of Books.

But I think this is really a kind of slum of philosophy. It is not acceptable that in the era of Russell, Wittgenstein and Frege, people can write such sloppily constructed work. I guess they can get away with it because they don't primarily address technically competent philosophers. They tend to address people in other disciplines such as literary theory. And also, there's always a kind of fringe element in philosophy that thinks, "Well, we shouldn't just try to do our subject in this narrow way. We should be open to all these other ideas." I am all in favor of openness to new ideas but I think you have to make a distinction between serious high level philosophical work and work that is intellectually unacceptable.

"I once said this to Michel Foucault, who was more hostile to Derrida even than I am, and Foucault said that Derrida practiced the method of *obscurantisme terroriste* (terrorist obscurantism). We were speaking French. And I said, "What the hell do you mean by that?" And he said, "He writes so obscurely you can't tell what he's saying, that's the obscurantism part, and then when you criticize him, he can always say, 'You didn't understand me; you're an idiot.' That's the terrorism part." And I liked that. So I when I wrote an article about Deconstruction, I asked Michel if it was OK if I quoted that passage, and he said yes.

Foucault was often lumped with Derrida. That's very unfair to Foucault. He was a different caliber of thinker altogether."

From *Reason magazine* - February 2000. Reality Principles: An Interview with John R. Searle. By Edward Feser and Steven Postrel.

Philosophical enemies

G. F.:

There must be something of your personal style that gets you involved in these very confrontational exchanges with other philosophers. To take some examples, we had just talked about Derrida, and there is also the case of Daniel Dennett, among others.

John Searle:

I'm always puzzled by that. I may have a reputation for belligerence or pugnacity. I am not aware of any such impulse.

G. F.:

Dr. Maria Massone told me that in a philosophy conference in Chile, a couple of years ago, you climbed the stage when Maturana was speaking, in order to refute him.

John Searle:

I do have definite opinions about a lot of issues and I try to state them clearly. And if you do that, people get very upset. Certainly, Dennett got upset about strong artificial intelligence. And Derrida got upset. But I don't, in any sense, feel belligerent or hostile. I think they hate me much more than I hate them. I don't hate Dennett or Derrida. I feel sorry for Derrida, and I think Dennett is confused. But I detect in their writings about me, real passionate hatred. I don't feel that about them. If you look at my exchanges with Dennett, I'm very polite and he's not. He's just in a something of a frenzy.

What I say irritates them because they have false beliefs and I can show that they're false. But that's just how it is. That's what philosophy is like. That's what we're supposed to be doing. We're supposed to be trying to discover the truth and I think that Derrida, Rorty, and Dennett, to name three people who have more similarities than they would like to admit, I think they make great mistakes.

They're in show business and I'm not. I'm just trying to state the truth. And I've discovered that people get passionately upset if you point out that they're mistaken.

The harshest attacks on me are not over deconstruction, but over strong artificial intelligence. There's a whole army of people out there who built their professional careers on the ridiculous idea that by sitting at a computer typing in programs they're creating consciousness. They're creating a real mind. That's so silly, it's pathetic. But it's not enough to say it's pathetic. I can refute it with a specific argument. And when you refute it, they don't say, "Oh, well, that's very nice. Now we can go do something else." No. They say, "You must be mistaken. This is terrible." And they get very excited and very upset.

Continental and Anglo-Saxon Philosophy

G. F.:

How do you see now the Continental philosophical scene as opposed to the Anglo American?

John Searle:

Well, I don't know this topic well enough to have a really good understanding of it. But I think it's a mistake to think there's an opposition between Continental philosophy and Analytic philosophy. There are some very good analytic philosophers on the European continent. There's a bunch in Paris, and there's a whole lot in Scandinavia, Germany, Italy, and so on. When I go and lecture in all these countries, I have no problem finding intelligent people to talk to.

The idea of an opposition between Continental philosophy and Analytic philosophy is kind of a joke. It's as if you said there are two things that go on in the United States - business and Kansas. I mean it's a category mistake. "Analytic" names a method, and "Continental" names a geographical location. And, of course, all kinds of methods are followed in Europe.

I think there are at least three different kinds of philosophical methods I'm familiar with on the European continent. First there is there's the phenomenology tradition of Husserl, Heidegger, Sartre, and Merleau Ponty. There are some good things that come out of that. But mostly it's second rate for reasons I can explain to you. They don't have a rich enough theoretical apparatus. They don't have the methodological tools for logical analysis.

Then, there are straight analytic philosophers in Germany, Scandinavia and, to some extent, in France. They are also getting stronger in Italy. They tie their philosophy in with cognitive science, linguistics, and other disciplines.

And I think we'd have to recognize the Frankfurt school, neo-Marxist analysis of Habermas and others.

It's fascinating to see what happened to Marxism because, of course, Marxism was very influential in my childhood, especially in France. I am thinking of people like Sartre. And now I don't see that it has any vitality. People talk a sort of Marxist jargon, but it's mostly window dressing. I don't see any active Marxist movement in France, Germany or England.

Aesthetics

John Searle:

Maybe when Aristotle said that the greatest genius is being able to think up poetry, he was thinking of poetic metaphors. Modern poetry has set itself a very difficult task. In a way, it's much harder than traditional poetry. The aim of modern metaphor is to take an experience you have, and construct a verbal object so that anybody who reads that verbal object will have the same experience you did. And it may be an experience of watching raindrops hit a windowpane, or walking next to a river. And now, construct a verbal object such that somebody who reads the poem will have your experience. And that's an impossible job, but it's interesting to see how good poets try to do it.

G. F.:

Are you thinking of someone?

John Searle:

Well, the other day, I got a gift from a student. She gave me a book of poems by a woman named Amy Clampitt. And my research assistant started reading this and said, "it's terrible." So I picked it up and read a poem aloud. And I thought it was absolutely stunning. It was just gripping, "how did she do this?" My research assistant thought this should be a traditional poem. It ought to have rhyme, and there ought to be a story that it tells, and so on. And I tried to explain to her this poet sets herself a task which is quite different from the poetry you're familiar with. She wants to create a verbal object. It doesn't have to rhyme. It has to be a verbal object so when you read it, you will have the experience that she had before she created that object. And it's fascinating to see how she does that. So, in the end, I came to the conclusion that she's a pretty good poet. That's the first time I read her.

Gustavo Faigenbaum

G. F.:

Surrealists would have a totally different approach to poetry.

John Searle:

I think that's a different case. It began with Baudelaire's disordering of the senses. This is part of the problem with modern art forms. They have to constantly be pushing against the tradition and against the limitations. But there's nothing to push against anymore. And this means that a large part of what is out there, is just trash. It's so sad. You see, part of great art is overcoming the obstacles created by the medium, in order to achieve the artistic objective. Now, in the Renaissance, there was a tremendous flowering as people overcame the difficulties of creating a visual likeness of a three-dimensional object on a two-dimensional surface. And they mastered perspective. And they mastered all kinds of devices of the illusion. But once the representational component was gone, and once there was no limit set by the medium explored, then the internal discipline collapsed. That is, I think Western art is right now in rather poor shape.

258

I taught once in Rome and I stayed at the American Academy, which is mostly full of young artists. And they staged an exhibit. And the exhibit was rather touching in its *pathos*. So, for example, a typical exhibit would be, somebody would put items on the staircase. They'd put an orange, and then a slipper and then a sock, and then an orange, and then a slipper and then a sock. This is supposed to be a work of art. And I spoke to one of these people and I said, "It must be great for you to be in Rome with all this great art that's in Rome," and she said, "No, it's very depressing because, how can we compete with that? We look at these great paintings of the past and we can't compete with that." What they do is they arrange socks and oranges and so on. It's sad.

Not everybody does that. I have a friend who is a major artist. His name is Ronny Kitaj. He's what they call a figurative painter. He can actually paint paintings that look like people or like houses. I'll show you one in my house. So, not everybody is trapped into the post-modernist genre. But it seems to me it's very limited. There's not an awful lot you can do with it. I think most abstract expressionism is very limited. I cannot imagine that future generations will find, let's say, Mark Rothko, a very powerful painter. You've got a blotch of one color and a blotch of another color.

259

Well, there are others that I think are better, like Motherwell, or Larry Rivers, who paints the French money.

My experience as a speech act theorist had a bad effect on my artistic sensibilities in the following way. I had always found abstract expressionism, abstract art, fairly appealing. But once I set down to write an article about pictures – how do pictures work? What kind of speech act is a picture? What can you do with pictures? And I wrote an article, but I never published it because I wasn't completely happy with it. Maybe I'll take it up again. In the course of this, while I was trying to describe how pictures work and how you convey content on a two-dimensional surface, I conceived a passionate hatred of abstract painting. It was almost irrational. Maybe it was irrational that I saw the difficulties facing Daumier, Rubens, Renoir or Manet as such tremendous difficulties, and how they overcame those difficulties; and it seemed to me that when you get to people like Rothko, that they made life easy for themselves.

I remember going to the Chicago Art Institute while I was writing this article and down in the basement they had all the contemporary abstract expressionists. I thought, "That's where you bastards belong – down in the basement." It was a stupid and irrational reaction on my part. So it's the only time when my work on speech acts actually had an obvious effect on my esthetic reaction.

American Universities

G. F.:

What is your perception of American universities today?

John Searle:

There was a remarkable thing that happened at the end of the Second World War. We began to develop a very high level of intellectual achievement in the research universities. There was a period – I'm not sure that it continues – when the United States led the world in most of the subjects that I know anything about – in psychology, philosophy, linguistics, and many others. In a large number of subjects the United States really was the best in the world. And the best universities in the world were in the United States.

I think that's probably less true now. I think we suffered from the decline in public confidence after the 1960's, when there was less funding for universities here. Also, in many parts of the world, universities are getting better. It's a good thing that

Gustavo Faigenbaum

we'll be getting more competition from other countries.

We're no longer in this golden age that we had when there was funding and when there was a great deal of optimism. Yet, I think the universities are still very healthy. I think that we were in a better position to survive the assaults on the university system made in the 1960's and 1970's, than was the case in a lot of European countries, where they abandoned some of the traditional structure of academic authority, and allowed students to participate in decisions about who gets hired and things like that. The basic institutional structure of the American university was not seriously challenged by the upheavals of the 60's and 70's. The structure goes on as before. Then it becomes a question of funding and commitment.

The real problem I have with my colleagues is that I think a lot of professors are not really serious. They have an easy life. They go down to the campus, give their lecture, get their paycheck, and go home. But they don't work desperately hard. They're not desperately trying to discover the truth.

I've been a professor for a long time, and I have to tell you... I don't want to overstate it, but it's hard to be a professor without having at least a little bit of contempt for, or without having a certain amount of

262

disappointment in, the profession; because many academic professionals don't realize what a privileged position they're in. They don't take advantage of this wonderful opportunity they have. It's just another job and they get their money and they teach the students and they go home. But they're quite cynical about the university, the ideals of higher education, the students, and what they're trying to do.

So, at some level, I think you can't be a professor and do a good job without having negative feelings about many other professors. A lot of them are just lazy people who don't really work hard. And I'm extremely depressed by that. People are not really committed to getting the truth, and they're not committed to trying to teach their students.

I'm trying to state the truth and to get it across to these kids. Now, a lot of my colleagues don't much care. They don't care about the education of the students.

The philosophy that is coming

John Searle:

Something is quietly happening under our very noses, which I think is the next great transformation in philosophy. Modern philosophy, beginning the 17th century, treated the existence of knowledge as problematic. And the Cartesian revolution in philosophy that went through Descartes, Francis Bacon, and on through Locke, Berkeley, Hume, Leibniz, Spinoza, Kant and Hegel and all the rest of it, to that enterprise, epistemology was central.

When Descartes started this revolution in the 17th century, the very existence of certain, objective, universal knowledge was very much in question. It was seen as very doubtful that you could have this type of knowledge. And there was a crisis produced by the conflict between the scientific knowledge of the 17th century, and traditional religion.

Today, that era is over. Knowledge is no longer problematic. The central intellectual fact about the contemporary world is that knowledge grows daily. There isn't any doubt about it. Pick up any textbook on chemistry or engineering, and you will see acres of knowledge, which is objective, certain, and universal. There just isn't any question about it. So the existence of knowledge is no longer problematic. And as a consequence, epistemology is no longer the center of philosophy. This is a wonderful development because it gives us the possibility of creating general theories of mind, language, and society – this is really what my work is – which are not based on the assumption that you have a desperate problem trying to overcome skepticism. I don't take skepticism seriously.

G. F.:

That means that you are not only committed to *ontological* realism, but also to *epistemological* realism.

John Searle:

That's right. Let me state this point precisely. I am not saying there is no place at all for the traditional philosophical skeptical worries, but I see them as like Zeno's paradoxes about space and time. So it's an interesting puzzle how I can get to the other side of the room ,if first I must go half the way, but before that I must go half of the half, and even before that, half of the half of the half. And so on ad infinitum. Yet, nobody seriously thinks I can't cross the room.

In the same way, I want to say it's a nice puzzle how I know I'm not dreaming, how I know I'm not a brain in a vat, how I know I'm not deceived by an evil demon, not having hallucinations, and all the rest of it. But nobody should seriously think that these puzzles challenge the existence of knowledge – that I can't know that water is made of hydrogen and oxygen, or that the earth is a satellite of the sun, or that the heart pumps blood. All of those things are known with certainty. We have just an overwhelming amount of information about those sorts of propositions. I think that you still have the puzzles, but they no longer are central to philosophy.

Now one other qualification I need to make is this –real life epistemology is alive. Real life epistemology is concerned with questions like these: How do you know that AIDS is caused by the HIV virus? How do you know that the population of California will continue to grow at the present rate? How do we actually verify our claims?

That, I think, is as alive and important as ever. And it should be, because with the advance of knowledge claims, we have to have systematic checks of the claims. So I don't, for a moment, suppose that the death of skepticism means that anything goes, that there's a kind of irrationality. But I do think that the tradition in which epistemology was the center of philosophy is now dead.

Paradoxically, I think Wittgenstein produced results that he would never have liked. That is, I think, by taking skepticism seriously and dealing with the skeptical objections, Wittgenstein has created the possibility of a kind of systematic philosophy, which he hated. He hated the kind of philosophy I do, where you try to get a systematic general theory of language or of mind. He thought, "No, you just solve philosophical puzzles, such as those about skepticism, and you do it by describing the language games." And what I'm saying is, "No, now that's over. The era of skepticism is over. We can now create systematic, theoretical structures."

Now what is funny about all this is that at a time when knowledge grows daily, at a time when there isn't any doubt that any textbook of computer science, mechanical engineering or organic chemistry just contains a huge amount of knowledge, there is this sort of Greek chorus of people on the sidelines, the post-modernists shouting, "We don't really know anything! There isn't even any definite meaning! It's just *la textualité du texte*!"

G. F.:

Or, it's all a matter of power.

John Searle:

Yeah. That's right. It's all a matter of power and oppression. And I think there's something slightly

267

Gustavo Faigenbaum

absurd about the post-modernist who buys an airplane ticket on his laptop, gets on an airplane, flies to a distant city, is driven in a taxicab to a lecture hall, and then gives a lecture over a loudspeaker system saying, "We have no knowledge. Claims to knowledge are just oppressive devices." It's too funny for words.

G. F.:

That's a pragmatic contradiction.

John Searle:

Yeah. There is something slightly ridiculous about this.

John Searle's method

G. F.:

Is there something like Searle's method of doing philosophy?

John Searle:

I don't think so. I have used different methods for different tasks. When I did the theory of speech acts, I tried to analyze the necessary and sufficient

268

conditions for the performance of a speech acts and the utterance of a sentence. And that was a kind of classic method of analytic philosophy - get necessary and sufficient conditions.

In a way, I applied that to the study of intentionality. There, the question was not necessary and sufficient conditions for the performance of an action, but the necessary and sufficient conditions for an intentional state to be satisfied - the conditions of satisfaction. That gave me the analysis of meaning, because I got that in terms of the imposition of conditions of satisfaction on conditions of satisfaction. The method is a kind of logical analysis.

When you apply it to institutional reality, the question there is, "Well, what fact about this piece of paper makes it a dollar bill? And what fact about this collection of buildings here makes this the University of California?" And that's what led me to the analysis of institutional reality.

So, in a way, the basic method is always to try to examine the structure of the facts. What is it to have a belief? What is it perform a speech act? What is money? What is property and marriage? So there is a kind of method, but it is not a secret technique. It's just the method of logical analysis. And if you get something that just looks obviously

Gustavo Faigenbaum

false, you know you have probably made a
mistake. That's where I really think I differ from a lot
of people that write on the philosophy of mind. They
get ridiculous results like we don't really have
consciousness, or there's no such thing as
intentionality, or when we say we have belief we're
really just talking about a manner of speaking, it's
just an intentional stance. If you get such a result,
then you know you made a mistake. So I try to
avoid saying things that are false and you'd be
surprised what a difference that makes.

G. F.:

Now when you're doing this kind of logical
analysis in a wide sense, an important part of it
seems to be to pick up the paradigmatic case to
analyze. For example, in order to study institutional
reality, you take money, marriage, the state.

John Searle:

You always take clear examples. When I did
speech acts, I took the example of promising,
because it's a very clear example. If you just took
one of Austin's verbs like "remark," and tried to
analyze what makes something a remark, it's much
harder, because it's much more vague and I don't
think it names a well defined type of speech act.
Whereas, "promise" clearly does. So always start

270

with very clear examples where there isn't any question about whether or not you have an institutional fact, or a speech act, or an intentional state, and then analyze its logical structure.

G. F.:

You also use a lot of nice illustrations when you lecture. I thought that students would see that as a trait of your personality, and they might think, "that comes out naturally for him." And they wouldn't think there is a whole method behind such systematic examination of examples, counter-examples, and borderline cases.

John Searle:

I do have an unintended effect on students and on some colleagues. A lot of people have the impression that it's very easy for me, that I find philosophy very easy. A good friend of mine who's a very good philosopher said, "When you write a book you just sit down and pour it out." They think that I have this big bucket and I just pour it on the page. They don't realize how hard it is. And the same happens with the students. I come in and give a lecture and they think, "Well, for him it's very easy." But it's not. That's a mistake.

271

If you try to state things very clearly and very simply, it looks easy. But it's precisely because it's so difficult, and you struggle with the difficulties, that if you work hard enough, and try hard enough, you can eventually state your results very simply and clearly. But the clarity and the simplicity are the result of an enormous labor. And the paradox is that people think clarity and simplicity are a sign of the absence of labor. It's exactly the reverse. I said in one of my books that I have a very simple principle, "If you can't say it clearly, you don't understand it yourself." But the ability to say it clearly takes an enormous amount of work.

A lot of people, even professionals, have the impression, "Well for you philosophy is real simple and you just sort of say it and then go home and have a beer. And it's not real work for you." And that's wrong. It's very difficult. And it's precisely because it's so difficult, and I work so hard at it, that I can in the end say what I want to say in a simple way.

G. F.:

Would you say that you do some kind of phenomenological analysis of the examples you take?

John Searle:

The aim is different from phenomenology. To my amazement, when a lot of people saw my book on intentionality, they thought I was trying to do phenomenology, that I was trying to do was Husserl did. And that's not true at all. Husserl was trying to examine the structure of consciousness. So was Heidegger in *Being and Time*. I am not. I am trying to analyze the conditions of satisfaction on mental states. There is an overlap. Sometimes, to get at the mental states you have to take the cases where they're conscious. But the actual formal analysis is independent of consciousness.

I start with what we know about the world: the world consists of entities described by physics and chemistry. I start with the fact that we're products of evolutionary biology, we're biological beasts. Then I ask, how is it possible in a world consisting entirely of brute facts, of physical particles and fields of force, how is it possible to have consciousness, intentionality, money, property, marriage, and so on? Heidegger, for example, starts with *being in the world*. He starts with the situation of *Dasein* in the world. And for me that's a mistake. You'll be led to some kind of idealism and I think you can't make sense of either Husserl or Heidegger unless you see that they are idealists in a very profound sense, since they think the human experience is somehow

273

Gustavo Faigenbaum

more fundamental than physical reality. But physical reality is what's fundamental.

"Philosophy is, in part, the name for a whole lot of subject matters that we really don't know how to settle the issues in, where we don't have established methods for resolving questions. Now for me that's part of the fun, it's wide open. You're not hemmed in, you're not trapped in a narrow little research program. But a lot of people find that uncomfortable, that you can't fall back on an established body of philosophical truths. Okay, now you have this wide-open area, but as soon as we can get a question into a precise enough form that it admits of a systematic answer that everybody can see is right, we quit calling it philosophy. We call it science or mathematics or logic.

So once you have the method of coming up with answers, it's time for you to close up shop as a philosopher."

From John Searle Interview: Conversations with History; Institute of International Studies, UC Berkeley. (http://globetrotter.berkeley.edu/people/Searle/searle-con0.html)

G. F.:

Your book *Mind, Language and Society*, where you summarize the main tenets of your philosophical work, gives the impression that you

have that whole research program in your head
from the very beginning.

John Searle:

That's another thing. As I was telling you the
other day, in a sense you write one big book in your
whole life and each separate book is sort of another
chapter of the big book. But you don't know that
when you start. You don't have a draft. And you
don't see the implications.

When I wrote *Speech Acts* I didn't see the
implications for mind, society, or political
philosophy. You work it out as you go along. I was
very lucky. That is, I got off to a good start. I think I
was very lucky to work on speech acts, and to get a
pattern of analysis that worked well elsewhere. I
happened to be at a certain place at a certain time.
I studied with Austin and I had these ideas. And if
I'd been at a different place or another time, it might
not have worked. Your first book is very important
because, if it's successful, your other books can
build on that.

G. F.:

Maybe if you had stayed in America you would
be working on the digital computer model of mind.

John Searle:

(Laughing) I don't know. I think I was very lucky that my first book provided a foundation for my other books. And I didn't know that at the time. There's a sense in which I was almost sleepwalking when I wrote *Speech Acts*. I really didn't know what I was doing, but it just seemed the right way to go.

When I published it, I felt like "it's probably hopeless," "it's probably stupid." And I couldn't bear to read reviews of it. I never read the reviews. It was only a long time after I had published it, that I could actually read it and feel good about it.

G. F.:

Was the acceptance of the book immediate?

John Searle:

No, I was told the reviews were very hostile. There was a review by a linguist in *Language* that was negative. Philosophers that I knew told me, "Well, you know, maybe it's all right, but it's not real philosophy. Real philosophy is about big questions. Real philosophy is not about speech acts." And the logicians sneered at it. They thought, "Speech acts? That's ridiculous." They didn't see any formulae or truth tables. "What kind of logic is this?" There was general hostility.

Then, it became a classic. It got translated into a lot of languages, it influenced people in other disciplines, and it began to be understood. After twenty years it got translated into all kinds of other languages - in Russian, in Eastern European languages, in Japanese. It had an influence beyond anything I ever expected.

This is, by the way, one of the great satisfactions of our profession. Last week I went into a bookstore and I saw a new printing of *Speech Acts*. It suddenly occurred to me that people buying this book were not born when I wrote it. Just think about that. The people who buy and read the book today didn't exist when I wrote the book in the 1960's. And that, I think, is a wonderful thought because it means I am now writing for people who aren't yet born. There's a difference between journalism and us. Journalism has to succeed today. If it doesn't succeed today, it's finished. But, in our profession, you can write a book and it can keep going, and going, and building.

The book acquires a life of it's own. I don't feel that I have to defend *Speech Acts* or any other book. They can stand on their own.

Gustavo Faigenbaum

In 1971 I went to give some lectures in Germany. When I arrived at the railway station I looked in the railway station bookstore. I wasn't looking for any books by me, and there was a copy of *Speech Acts* in German. *Sprechakte*. And I had this sudden thought. I thought, "My first-born child can speak German."

It's ridiculous, but that's what I thought. I thought, "Now this book has to stand on it's own. It's now grown up. I don't have to defend it or clarify it. It's got it's own life."

G. F.:

I think that's a very nice way to finish. Thanks so much.

John Searle:

Well, thank you very much Gustavo. You do a great job. I really appreciate it.